# RETHINKING ECCLESIA

## Being and Becoming Christ Communities: Towards a Borderless Church

### Liturgical, Missiological and Prophetic Diaconal Perspectives

# RETHINKING ECCLESIA

## Being and Becoming Christ Communities: Towards a Borderless Church

### Liturgical, Missiological and Prophetic Diaconal Perspectives

EDITORS
Daniel Rathnakara Sadananda
Solomon Paul J.

CHURCH OF SOUTH INDIA
2021

**Rethinking Ecclesia - Being and Becoming Christ Communities: Towards a Borderless Church - Liturgical, Missiological and Prophetic Diaconal Perspectives** - Jointly Published by the Indian Society for Promoting Christian Knowledge (ISPCK), Post Box 1585, Kashmere Gate, Delhi-110006 and The Church of South India (CSI), CSI Centre, No. 5, Whites Road, Royapettah, Chennai - 600 014.



*Online Order: http://ispck.org.in/book.php*

ISBN: 978-93-90569-15-1

*Laser typeset by*

**ISPCK,** Post Box 1585, 1654, Madarsa Road, Kashmere Gate, Delhi-110006 • *Tel:* 23866323

*e-mail:* ashish@ispck.org.in • ella@ispck.org.in
*website:* www.ispck.org.in

# Contents

# Acknowledgements

Rethinking Ecclesia publication is a result of well thought and planned series of 8 consultations in the year 2018. These consultations are indeed a historical moment in the history of CSI as we commemorated 70 years of faithful journey and Reformation 500. All the papers presented and the meaningful conversations helped the Church of South India to engage more vigorously in the process of searching new theological directions and visions as CSI steps into a new decade.

The theme "Being and becoming Christ communities – towards a borderless Church" were discussed from a) Biblical perspective, b) theological and ethical perspective, c) liturgical and missiological perspective, d) prophetic and diaconal perspective, e) empowerment and educational perspective, f) healing and reconciliation perspective, g)National and global ecumenical perspective.

The Moderator of the Church of South India, Most Rev Thomas K Oommen, who inaugurated these consultations, remarked that the theological exercise of Rethinking Ecclesia consultations has helped the Church to find new directions in the pilgrim journey of CSI. He said that these explorations should continue to challenge the church and its mission and also make way for newer forms of ministerial engagements with the people at the grassroots.

These consultations has enabled the church to make a theological audit of CSI, create a network of theological educators who are CSI and gave opportunity for the seminary and the church to bridge the existing gaps in working closely with one another for the sake of a united mission.

This book is a compilation of articles presented during the Biblical and Theological perspective consultations held at CSI Synod, Chennai. Biblical scholars and theologians of CSI came and presented their insights on the theme.

At this moment we thank the God of koinoinia who called CWM to partner with CSI from the beginning till the end of this Rethinking Ecclesia consultations helping us to encourage each other and also assuring us of God's accompaniment in our Pilgrim journey.

I also place my thanks to the Youth Department of CSI for their meticulous efforts in planning and implementation of these consultations and coordination in bringing out this publication.

Special thanks to ISPCK for publishing these books and partnering with CSI in continuance of God's mission.

**Rathnakara Sadananda**

# Preface

It is with great joy and contentment that I present the book – **Rethinking Ecclesia: Being and Becoming Christ Communities - Towards a borderless Church**, a series of articles deliberating on the theme from National and Global Ecumenical perspectives.

Borders have become an undeniable reality today. Both the nation-state and the Church are governed by borders. If borders are to offer security and protection, the same borders also exclude or de-mark the other. The Church in India, since many decades now has been struggling to engage with the many identity-markers such as caste, region, denomination, tradition, gender and so on… Though the Church is called to live and profess the liberating Spirit of God which transcends borders yet, she is engaged in grappling with the many challenges imposed by the identity-markers.

These identity-markers which promote intrinsic value to the worth of an individual and betterment of the community have become a strong border/barrier among communities leading to negation of life. It is in this context that the book "Rethinking Ecclesia" tries to find meaning and sense for the existence of the CSI today and tomorrow.

The articles in this book resonate the visions, dreams, aspirations and even frustrations in re-imaging a new community centered on Christ and show the way forward towards a borderless Church. These articles are not ashamed of the grave mistakes the Church has committed in stiffening borders and building walls of animosity, but have rather lamented over them in repentance, waiting for another opportunity to set it right through theological articulations. They reflect on the present context of the Church battling even more greater hurdles as the socio-geo-political climate of the nation is going through a shift towards rightist ideological forces.

"**Rethinking Ecclesia**" is the result of a well-thought and planned series of eight consultations in the year 2018. These consultations were indeed a historical moment in the history of CSI as we commemorated 70 years of faithful journey and Reformation 500. All the papers presented, and the meaningful conversations helped the Church of South India to engage more vigorously in the process of searching for new theological directions and visions as the CSI steps into a new decade.

The theme "**Being and becoming Christ communities – towards a borderless Church**" were discussed from a) Biblical, b) Theological, c) Liturgical and Missiological, d) Prophetic Diaconal, e) Empowerment and Educational, f) Health, Healing and Harmony as well as g) National and Global Ecumenical perspectives. Around 109 papers were presented during these consultations containing voices from within and outside, voices of complement and voices of dissent, voices from the vulnerable and those in responsible positions.

The Moderator of the Church of South India, Most Rev Thomas K. Oommen, who inaugurated these consultations, remarked that the theological exercise of Rethinking Ecclesia consultations has helped the Church to find new directions in the pilgrim journey of CSI. He said that these explorations should continue to challenge the Church and its mission and also make way for newer forms of ministerial engagements with the people at the grassroots, especially in liberating the weak and the oppressed.

These consultations affirmed that the Church is the sign and the sacrament of the reign of God; that as the continuation of the incarnation and an instrument of the reign of God, the Church ventures to live out her commitment and faith as an alternative, that proclaims boldly that another world is possible, right here and now in our midst; and that the Church is the penultimate, subject to change and transformation till she is ultimately absorbed into the very reign of God. And therefore, the consultations were indeed a prophetic call to rethink *ecclesia*, not only its significance, importance and relevance, but also its being and becoming.

These consultations have enabled the Church to make a theological audit of CSI, create a network of theological educators in the CSI and provide opportunity for the theological faculties and the Church to bridge the existing gaps in working closely with one another for the sake of a united mission. Consultations also provided the much-needed space for the Church and the theological fraternity to listen to, have dialogue with one another, and work together to overcome the lacuna that exists between the seminary and the sanctuary.

This book is a compilation of articles presented during the consultations from **Liturgical, Missiological and Prophetic Diaconal Perspectives** held at CSI Synod, Chennai. Theologians involved in the field of Liturgy, Mission and Diakonia presented their insights on the theme. The opinions and theological assertions expressed in the articles are of the authors themselves, put forth with sincere faith and hope that they would help the people of God to clearly and relevantly articulate the self-understanding of being and becoming Ecclesia.

Heartfelt thanks to the Moderator of CSI, Rt. Rev. Thomas K. Oommen, Deputy Moderator, Rt. Rev. V. Prasada Rao, and Treasurer, Adv. C. Robert Bruce for their immense solidarity and leadership during all the consultations that took place. Special thanks to the General Secretary, Rev. Dr. Daniel Rathnakara Sadananda, who was responsible for this theological exploration and exercise, without whose guidance, these consultations and this publication would not have been possible.

We thank the God of *koinoinia* who called the CWM to partner with CSI from the beginning till the end of these "Rethinking Ecclesia" consultations by helping us to encourage each other and also assuring us of God's accompaniment in our pilgrim journey towards becoming a borderless Church.

I also place my thanks to Mrs. Augustina Margaret, staff, Youth Department, CSI for her efforts in planning and implementation of these consultations and for coordinating to bring out this publication. Thanks to Mrs. Jessica Richard and Mrs. Angel Merlin for their help in proof reading and special thanks to ISPCK for publishing these books and partnering with CSI in the continuance of God's mission.

**Epiphany, 2020**
**Chennai, India**

**Solomon Paul J.**
**Editor**

Concept Note

# Towards a Borderless Church

At the time of independence in August 1947, the colonial masters re-drew the borders of our nation even as it wriggled in pain and tension. People began to move to safer places, many were displaced from their habitats and lives and livelihoods lost. The country paid dearly for its independence. In September 1947, our fore-fathers and mothers decided to overcome the borders of denominational faith, mission allegiance and regionalism to form the Church of South India. Inspired by the Lord's prayer for unity and oneness 'that they all may be one as we are one', our fore-fathers and mothers ventured into a radical discipleship of imitating God's oneness. To a divided India, to the divided church worldwide, the Church of South India became a parable of unity, a beacon of hope, an aroma of the Gospel.

Borders do exist. Each cell in our body has a border. However, each cell communicates and interacts with the other. Every one of us lives within certain borders and ever-widening borders, within the borders of our home, family, congregation, faith communities, village, town, state, and country. At times we share borders, we cross borders, we merge borders, we re-draw borders. We dream of borderless-ness. Thus, we live with borders, yet we yearn for borderless-ness. In our quest to understand borders and borderless-ness, we learn to understand the energy, power, potentials and the possibilities and opportunities that evolve in crossing and going beyond our borders.

A borderless Church calls us to look intently at our borders. Normally, borders are identity markers. Borders do inform us about what we are and what we are becoming. Anglican, Presbyterian, Congregationalist, and Methodist Christians in Southern India decided to redraw their ecclesial borders together to form, very consciously, a united and uniting Church of national and cultural identity. They indeed looked intently on the form of their faith, spiritual expressions, traditions, spiritual practice and how they organised themselves as congregations and churches. The varied faith expressions, spirituality, and liturgical traditions mingled together in their many-ness, yet interwoven into a colourful and powerful expression of oneness. The borders merged, were redrawn, new borders emerged.

In the first creation story, borderless-ness and harmony are evident. The varied, multiple forms and creatures created multitudes of borders that were held together in oneness and wholeness, an intrinsically connected, networked, harmonious blend is seen as good, and very good, culminating in Sabbath, the Shalom. Only the second creation story speaks of the process of self-discovery in relation to the other - in holding the other in respect and dignity, the identity of each is defined, interpreted and enhanced. The concept of identity formation, freedom with responsibility is introduced in the narrative only to affirm that when identity is misrepresented, and when the creature tries to impersonate the Creator, the connections, bonds and networks get destroyed.

The call and election narratives in the Old Testament are an invitation to understand this complex, yet beautiful interrelatedness and intrinsic value. The narratives of Abraham, Sarah and Hagar, Isaac and Rebecca, Esau, Jacob, Leah and Rachel show that they are invited to cross borders, share borders, draw new borders, and understand the mysteries beyond their borders and become a borderless community. For the writers of Genesis, their histories inform us of God's initiative that challenges human community to rediscover, reinvent and remember the borderless creation and be part of God's Shalom.

The story of Exodus is about breaking the borders that exploit and are oppressive. It is a story of empowerment for liberation; crossing the red sea - a baptism in water, is the visual symbol of overcoming borders and becoming a liberated community, a parable of liberation. The liberated community was called to represent the possibility of another world, where the world can hear its breathing and visualise its being. The commandments and the book of the covenant were given in order to make an alternative, another world possible, it was drawing new borders that would negate the borders that exploit, oppress, destroy and threaten life and proclaim the coming of justice and peace, not only within the borders of the liberated community, but beyond its borders and everywhere. Love, faithfulness, peace, justice, and righteousness are to be seen and experienced within the liberated community in order that it becomes the Gospel to the whole world.

The Deuteronomic eucharistic prayer (*anamnesis* - Deut. 26:5-10) holds together the wandering Aramean walking from the margins, crossing borders, the small and insignificant, few and negligible, strangers and aliens becoming empowered, to go through the struggles, pains, and sufferings, getting liberated from the crushing clutches of death and destruction to emerge as a people. It is a narration of resilience and resurrection, a living experience of breaking the chains of bondage and enslavement, to redraw borders that seem to extend and expand unceasingly.

The Prophetic literature which came at the time of exilic and post exilic period clearly depicts the community that was called to be an alternative, liberated community, which by losing its way and its borders emerged from its struggles of being conquered and occupied. The prophetic voice makes it clear that when the community loses its vision of liberation, corruption and injustice extinguish the power to move, connect and be open, when the community loses its dynamism and becomes static; connectivity, networks, and the power to transcend are destroyed and in the process people get marginalised and lose the creative power to overcome the borders and transcend the borders. Therefore, the prophetic call comes first as comforting, then as sowing the vision of a new heaven and new earth, but with a strong inclination to empower the community against corruption, injustice, oppression, and exploitation, so that they may discern and embrace the new that is already there and sprouting. Only in empowering the marginalised, in drawing out the inherent, innate, and immanent potentials, does the community once again regain movement, connectivity, and openness.

In the New Testament, Jesus' understanding of God as is defined in his conversation with the Samaritan woman is very instructive and profound - "God is Spirit; those who worship him must worship him in Spirit and truth" (Jn.4.24). God does not belong to one community, he is not stationary at Jerusalem or in Shechem, on the mount; God cannot be bound to certain traditions and forms of spirituality; he is boundless and borderless.

Jesus was preaching the reign of God, its imminence, and the reign of God, not the Church, was at the centre of his teaching. The reign of God is the safe space, that comforts, cares, heals and reconciles. It is a place where one receives forgiveness, grace, and loving kindness. The reign of God is where one rests powerlessness, vulnerability, frailty, weakness, insufficiency, and gets empowered. The reign of God calls the excluded, rejected, oppressed and outcastes, embraces them into an inclusive solidarity, to offer justice and peace. The reign of God is love, joy and hope, that brings integrity, wholeness, and harmony. It is the space and place where people experience the presence and accompaniment of God. The reign of God that Jesus proclaimed therefore, is not only borderless, but that which also gives assurance of eternity.

To make God's reign felt and experienced by commoners, Jesus' movement was evolved within the borders of Jewish religion. Jesus called out (*ecclesia*) twelve/seventy and created a community within the community. On this rock, I will build my Church (Matt.16.18), a rock-like, solid faith; but unlike the traditional understandings of messianic liberation, redemption was brought about by the suffering servant. Jesus standing firmly on the prophetic traditions of his faith, practiced prophetic *diakonia* as the means and instrument of liberation (Matt.16:21,24,25). Indeed, this was the culmination of a borderless, prophetic diaconal movement that moved from Nazareth to Gennesaret, to Tire Sidon, Samaria and to Jerusalem and back to Galilee. A borderless movement that empowered the margins, resisted the empire, critiqued religion and embraced the marginalised. It was a community called to be salt and light; a new life-giving and life-affirming movement, as flowing water and wind that blows wherever it pleases, a borderless new creation.

The Evangelists interpreted the crucified Christ as the one who draws all people to himself as he is lifted up. The crucified one, broken, crushed, and eliminated signifies the movement of the crucified people, and draws together those who are condemned to margins, denied of space, opportunity, rights and honour, bound because of their innocence and ignorance, excluded, made voiceless and unjustly persecuted. The crucified one in his passion and death enters the crucified communities and releases the power of life. The resurrected one who is boundless, and has overcome the limitations of time and space, inaugurates a new creation, boundless and borderless.

The early Church was indeed borderless, as it understood Jesus' command to go and make disciples of all nations (Matt.29:19), as a mandate to create borderless Christ communities. It also had a clear geographical strategy, 'you will be witnesses, in Jerusalem and in all Judea and Samaria and to the ends of the earth' (Acts 1:8). Peter also is 'converted' to the borderless Church, after the vision and real-life experience at Joppa and Caesarea (Acts 10). Paul, after his world-encircling, missional engagements writes his faith conviction; his *magna carta* "there is neither Jew nor Greek, slave nor free, male or female for you are all one in Christ" (Gal.3:28). It is very consistent with his sacramental theology which envisions a borderless Church, "Do you not know that all of us who have been baptized into Christ Jesus were baptized into his death? Therefore, we have been buried with him by baptism into death, so that, just as Christ was raised from the dead by the glory of the Father, so we too might walk in newness of life" (Rom.6:3,4). Every follower of Christ has been baptized into Christ, and therefore when he writes to Corinthians he clarifies that "The bread that we break, is it not a sharing in the body of Christ? Because there is one bread, we who are many are one body, for we all partake of the one bread" (1 Cor.10:16,17).

The ecclesiological reflections in the letter of Hebrews speaks of the visible and invisible Church. The language that 'we are surrounded by a great cloud of witnesses' (Heb.12:1), connects us with the Church of yesterday, with the Church of today and the future. The language used in the catholic epistles, of being strangers and pilgrims, to reflect the nature and being of the Church, depicts the struggles of living up to the great vision of a people of God. The theological affirmation that the Church is the Household of God (Eph.2:19) compared to the households of the time, and of the Church as God's House inform us about the profound theological affirmation: "Once you were not a people, now you are the people of God" (1Pet.2:10).

The eschatological vision of the book of Revelation depicts the New Jerusalem, the space of peace as an inclusive space, without borders. It speaks about a most valuable, yet fully transparent space, a space without a temple, as the whole space itself has the presence of God, which is light. All the nations of the earth will bring their splendor into it, it has gates that will always remain open, yet nothing impure will enter it (Rev.21:22ff). Even the heavenly space is not static; it is dynamic and transforming. The river of water of life, as clear as crystal flowing from the throne of God, and the trees of life which are for the healing and reconciliation of the nations, clearly affirm the process of being and becoming a Christ community, a borderless Church.

Today, we understand the Church as a sign and sacrament of the reign of God. She is an instrument of the reign of God and alternative that proclaims that another world is possible, that it is here and now in our midst. The Church is the penultimate, subject to change and transformation till she is absorbed into the reign of God. As a sign and sacrament of the reign of God, the Church has distinctive, discernible identity markers and borders, yet calling and exhorting people to the borderless reign of God.

As the Church of South India steps into the eighth decade of her being and becoming, may she be given grace upon grace to understand anew the gift of oneness and unity. May the 70-year celebrations be a sign of prophetic SEVA (*diakonia*), Social Empowerment - a Vision in Action upholding the sacramentality of life, where she, as a borderless Church travels beyond suspicion, fear and hostility in a multi-religious, multi-lingual, multi-cultural society. May she be empowered and emboldened to share, cross and redraw borders in order to set the energy of the margins, the crucified peoples free. May the children and the young be inspired to DARE into a process of Discernment And Radical Engagement, and be change makers and signs of transformation. May she be given grace to be a real MITHRA (friend) - Migrant Intervention Towards Holistic Responsive Action, to understand the beauty and significance of the small, frail and vulnerable, and be a movement of protest and resistance that gives DISHA, a new direction (Disability Intervention for Solidarity and Holistic Accompaniment), for those disabled, excluded, and condemned to margins. May the Church of South India be given grace to be God's instrument that brings dynamism and moves people, to connect not only with the Creator, but also with those around and all of God's creation, to open new possibilities of celebrating and living life in all its fulness. May the Church of South India be a new GEET, song (Gender Equity and Enabling Timetable), harmony that proclaims and practices equality, justice, and peace. In being and becoming a borderless Church, may the Church of South India open herself to God's eschaton, move in her radical engagement in the ever-continuous movement of unity and oneness of all and experience the fullness of Him who fills everything in every way (Eph.1:22), so that God may be all in all (1 Cor.15:28).

**Rev. Dr. D. Rathnakara Sadananda**

**General Secretary, CSI**

1

# Mission: Proclaiming the Borderless Reign of God

**Vincent Vinod Kumar**

The CSI Synod is commemorating the 500$^{th}$ anniversary of the Lutheran Reformation and 70$^{th}$ anniversary of the Church of South India with a series of consultations on *Rethinking Ecclesia* under the theme "Being and Becoming Christ communities – Towards a Borderless Church," providing us the opportunity to review in retrospect the journey of the CSI.

In this paper, we will first discuss the theme from a missiological perspective by highlighting the CSI's journey towards a borderless church. Second, we will look into the mission paradigm for the 21$^{st}$ century. Third, we will derive some approximate characterizations of the borderless church. Fourth, we will note the context and mission of the CSI. Finally, we will make some recommendations to the Church on how it should implement its mission strategies. The purpose of this paper is to help the CSI to discern the identity markers and to call and exhort people to the borderless reign of God.

## Journey Towards a Borderless Church

The CSI is an ecumenical Church, a united and uniting Church, moving forward with a dynamic vision for the communion of Churches in India. It is on a journey towards becoming a borderless Church, the Church in India throughout its history has usually been dependent on the churches of the West and it has always played an inconspicuous part in general Church history. The CSI, however, from its formative stage has played a leading role in ecumenism and has made a notable contribution towards unity in the Christian world.

The inspiration for the CSI came from ecumenism and the CSI's vision to fulfill the priestly prayer of Jesus Christ, the Lord of the Church, "That they all may be one, and that the world may believe that you have sent me" (John 17:21). The CSI aims to become an effective instrument of God's mission so that there will be greater peace, closer fellowship and fuller life in the Church and a renewed commitment for the proclamation of the Gospel of Jesus Christ through word and deed. The mission statement of the CSI reads,

> The Church of South India affirms that the Church is the Servant of God to carry on the mission rooted in Jesus Christ and based on the Scriptures. The Church through her mission expresses solidarity with the broken communities for a hope to face the challenges of life. The Cross continues to be the sign of hope for the witnessing Church, which strives towards Unity, Peace and Reconciliation as a vibrant Channel of God.[1]

Basically, the CSI is a union of episcopal and non-episcopal Churches. By classification, the CSI is a Protestant Church from the Reformed tradition, by orientation it is Anglican, and by polity it is episcopal. Historically, the CSI is the successor of the Church of England in India. It is a union of protestant churches that was formed on 27 September 1947 at St. George's Cathedral, Chennai. It is heartening to note that in the 1990s, a small number of Baptist and Pentecostal churches joined the union.[2]

The CSI is a church that seeks partnerships and relationships. The church accepts the Lambeth Quadrilateral as its basis and recognizes the historical episcopate in its constitutional form. It is one of four united churches in the Anglican Communion. The CSI has associations with the Anglican Communion, the World Council of Churches, the World Alliance of Reformed Churches, the Christian Conference of Asia, the Communion of Churches in India, and the National Council of Churches in India.[3]

The CSI was instrumental in establishing a Joint Council of the CSI, the Church of North India (CNI) and the Mar Thoma Church (MTC) in Nagpur in July, 1978. The preamble to the constitution of the Joint Council says,

> The Council has been constituted "as the visible organ for common action by the three churches, which recognize themselves as belonging to the one church of Jesus Christ in India, even while remaining as autonomous churches, each having its own identity of traditions and organizational structures."[4]

Following the formation of the Joint Council, the CSI, CNI, and MTC not only intercede for one another and observe the second Sunday in November every year as Festival of Unity, this commune of Churches is venturing into wider ecumenical relations to give witness to the One Lord Jesus Christ.[5]

Further, the CSI has always affirmed freedom and honesty in expressions of belief without allowing total individual subjectivity. It acknowledges that contemporary situations will warrant dynamism in the expression and interpretation of the faith.[6] A note in the *Basis of Union* states that,

> the uniting Churches accept the fundamental truths embodied in the Creeds named above (sc. Apostles' and Nicene) as providing a sufficient basis of union; but do not intend thereby to demand the assent of individuals to every word or phrase in them, or to exclude reasonable liberty of interpretation, or to assert that those Creeds are a complete expression of the Christian faith.[7]

In other words, the CSI acknowledges that social and cultural settings will legitimately play a dynamic role in shaping the confession of the Church, without thereby disregarding or disrespecting the profound traditions of the past.

Geographically, the CSI has been a borderless Church since its inception. The CSI has its base not only in the four southern states of India but also in the neighbouring country of Sri Lanka. The CSI also has congregations in north India and throughout the world. The CSI churches in north India are under the respective CNI bishops and the CSI churches in Europe are under the respective Anglican Bishops.

Theologically, the CSI sees itself only as a means for the mission of God and not an end in itself. From its very inception, the CSI did not think in terms of a long-lasting identity or static role. More radically, it saw for itself a transient nature and ever changing role as a borderless church. The Church was only a means toward the larger mission of God in the world.

R. D. Paul, one of the early interpreters of the self-understanding of the CSI, significantly makes the point that,

> The Church of South India does not imagine itself to be a Church which has been brought into existence in order that it may be one more Church among the various Churches in the world. The C.S.I., on the other hand, conceives of itself as being the means of bringing together other Churches, and that when the moment comes when other Churches would also unite, *it will dissolve itself in its present form, lose its present identity* and will agree to take its place in a bigger and larger united Church which would carry out God's will in the world....*It is willing to give up its identity and its constitution, if by so doing it can bring into being something even more in accordance with Christ's will for His Churches in the world* [8]

This vision of a Church is the strength of the CSI. To achieve this vision, a paradigm[9] of mission is necessary.

## Mission Paradigm Towards a Borderless Church

In its seventh decade of existence, the CSI is making a sincere effort at being and becoming a Christ community. An understanding of the 21st century paradigm of mission, therefore, will facilitate this process.

David Bosch in his book, *Transforming Mission*, while drawing attention to Hans Kung's six paradigms of mission, observes that a paradigm shift[10] in mission is taking place as the Church responds to new situations and challenges. As in the field of science, even in the Church there can exist an overlap of mission paradigms.[11] Paradigm shift in mission in one part of the world has an impact on missional thinking and practice all over the world resulting in new approaches and mission structures (i.e., modalities and sodalities).[12]

Viewing things from a logical perspective Bosch argues that, if "theology" is a reflective account of the faith, then "mission" is one of the expressions of the Christian faith. He reminds us that mission remains an indispensable dimension of the Christian faith and its purpose is to transform reality around it. Further, Bosch points out that mission should be understood as that dimension of our faith that refuses to accept reality as it is and aims at changing it by a continual process of shifting (paradigms), testing, discarding, and reformulating both its understanding and practice of mission. This is because mission is an enterprise that transforms reality. "Transforming mission" means both that mission is to be understood as an activity that transforms reality and that there is a constant need for mission itself to be transformed.[13] The broader understanding of the gospel compels the Church to be borderless expressing mission holistically, embracing all aspects of life. Expressing the collective opinion of Christian scholars regarding 21st century Christian mission, Bosch writes,

> Christianity in order to play a vital role in society, instead of looking for massive affirmations of faith which characterize the missionary enterprise of earlier times, it should witness in a chastened and humble manner to the supremacy of God in Jesus Christ.[14]

Regarding what Christian mission should do in the 21st Century, Bosch writes,

> Christian mission should take the best of modern science, philosophy, literary criticism, historical method, and social analysis, and constantly think through and rethink the theological understanding in the light of it all.[15]

It is heartening that the Church in the process of taking the best of everything in order to understand and practice mission has rediscovered the theology of mission of the first century that integrates faith and life, word and deed, proclamation and presence. This is termed "holistic mission." This Mission Paradigm evolves from a holistic understanding of Christian faith that is deeply rooted in the biblical theology of the Judeo-Christian faith of the Old and the New Testaments and is modeled by Jesus Christ himself. Describing Jesus' ministry Las G. Newman writes,

> In proclaiming the gospel, our Lord in his earthly ministry practiced and modeled a holistic approach to ministry. As the gospel writers recorded, he went throughout the towns and villages, "teaching in their synagogues, preaching the good news of the kingdom and healing every disease and sickness. When he saw the crowds, he had compassion on them, because they were harassed and helpless, like sheep without a shepherd" (Mat. 9:35-36). His ministry of teaching, preaching, healing, and compassion transformed human lives and restored human beings to the dignity of the *Imago Dei*. His gospel, expressed in word and deed, powerfully reconciled human beings to their creator in a living and vital relationship that not only impacted the individual but also families, communities and nations.[16]

This was the Christian gospel that was proclaimed in the first century, of the kingdom of God that is found to be universally transformative, strong, and holistic, and also challenging the *status quo* everywhere it is proclaimed. It was in this process of authenticating the biblical understanding of Christian mission as practiced in Jesus' ministry that an understanding of Christian mission as holistic, transformative and progressing toward a borderless Church has emerged.

Holistic mission is a comprehensive mission of the Church. If "conversion" is understood as "spiritual" and "liberation" as "political and economic," then "holism" can be understood as demanding mission to address not only the spiritual or the political or the economic aspects, but also the social and the theoretical aspects of every issue. The uniqueness of the concept of holistic mission is that, on one hand, it helps those who are engaged in authenticating the gospel in human conditions of poverty, and on the other, it tries to bring together both evangelical and ecumenical streams in Christianity.

The concept of Holistic Mission or Transforming Mission towards a borderless Church has a long history; it actually emerged from the concept of *Missio Dei* (God's mission).[17] This new image of mission led to an understanding that mission is participating in the movement of God's love toward people, since God is a fountain of love. Clarifying this new image of mission, Bosch writes,

> Mission is understood as having its origin in the heart of God. He is the source of mission. The missionary initiative should come from God. Secondly, the primary purpose of the missionary activities is interpreted as not simply planting of churches or saving of souls; rather, it has to be service to the "*missio-Dei*", representing God in and over against the world, pointing to God, holding up the God-Child before the eyes of the world in a ceaseless celebration of the feast of the Epiphany. It is also understood that the Church in its mission should witness to the fullness of the promise of God's reign and participate in the ongoing struggle between that reign and the powers of darkness and evil.[18]

Since God's concern is for the entire world, this should also be the scope of *Missio Dei*. It affects all people in all aspects of their existence. In other words, *Missio Dei* should be understood as God's transforming acts, and the missionary task of the Church should be taken to be as coherent, broad and deep as the needs and exigencies of human life.

## Some Approximations of a Borderless Church

Since 'mission' remains indefinable, the most we can hope for is to formulate some approximations of what mission is for a borderless Church.

1. Mission towards a borderless Church sees all generations of the earth as objects of God's salvific will and plan of salvation or, in New Testament terms, it regards the reign of God which has come in Jesus Christ as intended for all humanity.

2. It seeks to look at the world from the perspective of commitment to the Christian faith. This involves critical examination; for the sake of the Christian mission it will be necessary to subject every definition and every manifestation to rigorous analysis and appraisal. This involves challenging the evils of the status quo.

3. It gives expression to the dynamic relationship between God and the world (vertical and horizontal), particularly as this was portrayed, first, in the story of the covenant people of Israel, and then, supremely in the birth, life, death, resurrection, and exaltation of Jesus of Nazareth.

4. It considers the Bible as the source of Christian rule and practice of Christian faith but not as a storehouse of truths on which we draw at random. Mission practice towards a borderless church is not performed in un-broken continuity with the biblical witness; it is an altogether ambivalent enterprise executed in the context of tension between divine providence and human confusion. The Church's involvement remains an act of faith without earthly guarantees.

5. In this understanding of mission, the entire Christian existence is to be characterized as missionary existence. The Church begins to be missionary not through its universal proclamation of the gospel, but through the universality of the gospel it proclaims. Theologically speaking the Church is grounded in the gospel itself.

6. Mission towards a borderless Church is an affirmation of Christianity's solidarity with society. The mission, therefore, is the Church's missionary engagement in respect of the realities of injustice, oppression, poverty, discrimination, and violence.

7. Mission towards a borderless Church includes 'evangelism' as one of its essential dimensions. 'Evangelism' refers to the proclamation of salvation in Christ to those who do not believe in him, calling them to repentance and conversion, announcing forgiveness of sin, and inviting them to become living members of Christ's earthly community and begin a life of service to others in the power of the Holy Spirit.

8. The mission engagement in the transformation of the world does not imply blending with social and political movements to the point of becoming completely identified with them. The Church should not become a secularized Church. Nor should it engage only in soul saving and preparation of converts. It should faithfully articulate the Missio Dei.

9. Mission towards a borderless Church should be a sacrament and sign. It should be a sign in the sense of pointer, symbol, example or model. It should be a sacrament in the sense of mediation, representation or anticipation. This is because the Church lives in the creative tension of being called out of the world and sent into the world; it is challenged to be God's experimental garden on earth, a fragment of the reign of God, having "the first fruits of the Spirit" (Rom 8:23) as a pledge of what is to come (2 Cor 1:22). The ultimate goal of holistic mission is to bring the world under the reign of God.

10. In mission towards a borderless Church, the local church is "the people of God" in the local context or the Church-in-mission. This context and Church are part of the Church universal. As the present context comprises infinite diversities of contexts,

> the Church-in-mission has to have a multiple focus and creative mission strategies.[19]

Mission towards a borderless Church is, therefore, rooted in a specific spirituality or historic expression of faith. It is formulated in response to a specific social context and carried out with available resources. It addresses the body, mind, and spirit in human beings. It is a multifaceted ministry, in respect of witness, service, justice, healing, reconciliation, liberation, peace, evangelism, fellowship, church planting, contextualization, and much more.

## Context and Mission of the CSI

In its journey towards a borderless Church, the CSI is caught up in the changing contexts of society and it is imperative on our part to understand the function of the Church in our context. There are a wide variety of issues that we as a Church face today such as: globalization, poverty, corruption, illiteracy, inflation, marginalized people, issues of younger generations, new forms of social networking, problems of the aged, terminally ill, people living with HIV & AIDS, discrimination on the basis of class and gender, child labour, changing sexual ethics, issues of religious fundamentalism and minority rights, communalism, terrorism, naxalite rebels and so on.

As a missional response to these issues, the CSI, from its very beginning, has recognized the necessity of making periodical self-study of the issues it faces. Therefore, it maintains the practice of appointing Self-Study and Evaluation Commissions. Based on the recommendations of these commissions, the CSI monitors the course and direction of its life and witness and also faithfully strives to learn lessons from other churches in India and abroad, making necessary corrections to ensure the renewal and the advancement of the Church.[20]

The CSI Synod through its executive committee and synod meetings deliberates on the recommendations of the commissions and passes resolutions as the Church's verdicts. These resolutions are binding on all dioceses, congregations, Christian institutions, and individuals. These institutions of the CSI have to take all the resolutions as responsibilities bearing on their life and witness in their context.

The two CSI Synod Boards, namely, CSI Social Empowerment: Vision in Action (SEVA) (Diaconal Concerns) and CSI Board of Child Care (B.C.C) extends the Church's help and service to the needy regardless of their religious affiliations. The CSI SEVA strives to build a just, egalitarian society that is sensitive to gender issues and other inequalities through programs and projects such as sustainable development, community empowerment, sensitizing local congregations on social, economic, political, cultural and gender realities, building people's alliances and networking with movements on various campaigns related to human rights, and facilitating peace initiatives in the Church and conflict areas in South India. The CSI B.C.C empowers underprivileged children through partnership with *Kindernothilfe* (KNH) and other funding agencies and Churches around the world. The Board offers nurture and care programs to both children at risk and underprivileged children through Day Care Centers and Residential Care Programs. Other than SEVA and B.C.C, some of the CSI Synod ministries are Mission and Evangelism; Pastoral Concerns; Christian Education; Youth; Ecological Concerns; Communication; Dalit and Adivasi Concerns; EMS Liaison Office; CSI Women's Fellowship and the CSI Order of Sisters.

According to the 2012 CSI statistics, the CSI comprises more than four million members. Among these members, the majority live in rural areas as agricultural and farm related workers, small and marginal farmers or artisans. Another category of members are the coastal poor, linked to the fishing industry. A rural-urban divide exists in each of the 24 dioceses. A large section of CSI congregations comes from Dalit (SC) communities. Many of them are stigmatized as untouchables. Except for a small proportion of church members who are economically higher middle class, the majority are lower middle class people who are victims of structural injustices that causes among them deplorable levels of poverty, hunger and displacement. [21] Thus, in the footsteps of Jesus, the CSI has sought to serve the country in the field of education, a wide range of health care services, and development and social projects such as capacity building and empowerment programs. The CSI, however, cannot rest on her laurels. The Church has to recommit itself to being a borderless Church by taking a decisive stand in favour of the poor and marginalized.

## Recommendations for the CSI

The fundamental goal behind the initiative for the union of the churches in India was to promote effective evangelization and witness to the love of God in and through Christ in a nation of religious plurality. This mission should continue to be at the core of the CSI. The CSI's ministry and mission should be to create Christ communities that are empowered to produce a prophetic counterculture. K. C. Abraham says,

> In this situation the nature of the communities we seek has become an urgent concern. The Church should be at the service of people in their search for meaningful communities which are empowered to live in harmonious relationships with nature and between different faiths.... But our strategy should be to build smaller local communities which could be counter signs to existing society. It is likely that such counter communities could evolve out of our rural congregations where church life is not so distorted by the power wielders as in our urban congregations.... A genuine community should always be open to others in love. But the rootedness of the community in the faith of Jesus gives it a special character. Our attention should be on the identity and mission of the Church as a community or communities.[22]

In reviewing the CSI in its more than seven decades of existence, experimentation, and experience, what emerges is an enduring witness to its dynamic ecumenical selfhood. The Church should continue to strive to reverberate with the spirit of peace and concord in a world divided by borders.

The CSI in its pilgrimage— towards a borderless Church, in the first place, will have to look at itself. It should admit that oftentimes it has not succeeded in living up to Jesus' invitation to be the light of the world and the salt of the earth (Matthew 5:13-14). The Church leaders should dedicate themselves to leading an austere and prayerful life and inculcate in the members of the congregation the spirit of true contentment as against unbridled consumerism. The Church should first set in place its own systems to ensure transparency and accountability. To establish Christ communities, the Church must imitate the life and ministry of Christ.

The Church leaders should educate and implement the Church's diaconal concerns, which underline the centrality of the human person in all activities along with a commitment to the common good, aiming at the integral human development of all with a view to creating a just society.

Poverty and poverty-related problems are exacerbated by oppressive socio-cultural values and traditions. The CSI should carry out studies regarding harmful cultures, attitudes and practices, and designate ways to eliminate them. The Church should give top priority to teaching the Biblical worldview to counter oppressive socio-cultural values and traditions. Further, the Church should be an advocate for oppressed groups in all its local churches, institutions, and the society.

Despite attacks on the Church, the CSI should continue its work for the disadvantaged and marginalized and encourage the Church members who are doctors, lawyers and other qualified personnel to serve them. The Church should reach out to the least and the last of society.

The Church should inculcate the sacredness of human life from the very first moment of conception to its natural end in death. The Church leaders should educate the congregation members about female foeticide and baneful effects of substance abuse.

The Church should develop an education policy, which can draw on the Church's network of educational institutions as agents for social transformation, taking special care that the students imbibe ethical and spiritual values that will enable them to be citizens of our country who will serve the country with honesty, sincerity, integrity, commitment, and dedication.

Since one of the major causes of violence is injustice, the Church should commit itself to the liberation of weaker sections of society like tribals, women and dalits. In particular, the Church should reach out more to unorganized groups like fisher-people, farmers, migrants, domestic workers, victims of trafficking, and so on. More importantly, the Church should engage in advocacy and networking with NGO's and other like-minded groups and individuals dedicated to the cause of the poor. The Church should cooperate with the government in its efforts to improve the lot of the poor and help them gain access to the benefits and grants set aside in government schemes for them. The Church should be a voice for the voiceless and fight for their rights and privileges.

The Church must recognize that untouchability and caste discrimination are contrary to the Gospel of Jesus. The Church should root out this evil wherever it exists from within the Church, and make concerted efforts to empower dalits. The Church should commit itself to join hands with the dalits in their fight for equal rights and the constitutional benefits which are denied to them on the basis of religion. The Church should assure the marginalized and weaker sections that it will do everything possible to train and equip them for leadership positions at all levels.

The Church should stand for the protection of the environment. The Church should educate its members that humans are the stewards of God's creation and they must use all resources for the good of all, keeping in mind also the duty to future generations. Illegal mining, deforestation, some mega projects, pollution of water, air and land are destructive of ecology. The Church must resist such moves and encourage greater use of natural sources of energy, promote organic farming, encourage proper methods of waste management, and other such initiatives.

The Church should seize opportunities to be an instrument of reconciliation, seeking to be a bridge-building community among peoples. The Church should encourage its members, especially the small Christian communities, to engage in a dialogue of life whereby they interact with people of other religious traditions, being open to them, sharing their joys and sorrows. The Church should also encourage our faithful to enter into a dialogue of action whereby people of different persuasions work harmoniously with a common concern for the good of society.

The goal of building borderless Church with Christ communities cannot be achieved in isolation. The CSI should invite all sections of the CSI like pastors, heads of institutions, missionaries, church workers and church members to be fully involved in this noble endeavour. In the process of building Christ communities, the Church should encourage the youth, with their dynamism and vibrancy, to be involved in this task. The Church can never forget that it is not just by its efforts that a borderless Church can be built up. The Church should also pray for the realization of this goal.

The leaders of the Church in India should envision an India with more attributes of the kingdom of God such as justice and equity with their consequent fruits of love, peace and joy. The Church should entrust its efforts to build better India to Jesus, the Lord and Saviour, and imitate his integrity, compassion, selfless service and endurance.

## Endnotes

[1] *CSI Life,* Magazine of the Church of South India, Supplementary Issue for October 2017, Volume XV/Issue 10a, 127.

[2] CSI Synod, "History of Church of South India", < http://www.csisynod.com/> (14 October 2012).

[3] CSI Synod, "History of Church of South India", < http://www.csisynod.com/> (14 October 2012).

[4] J. R. Chandran (ed.), *The Joint Council of CSI – CNI – MTC – A Brief History and Interpretation* (Delhi: ISPCK, 1984) 43.

[5] J. R. Chandran, (ed.), *The Joint Council of CSI – CNI – MTC*, 39-44.

[6] Michael Hollis, *The Significance of South India* (London: Lutterworth, 1966), 38.

[7] As quoted in Hollis, *The Significance of South India*, 38.

[8] Rajaiah D. Paul, *The First Decade: An Account of the Church of South India* (Madras: Christian Literature Society, 1958), 9.

[9] The word 'paradigm' means "a pattern or model that stands for a set of assumptions, concepts, values, and practices that constitutes a way of viewing reality for the community that shares them especially in an intellectual discipline. *Online Free Dictionary*, <http://www.thefreedictionary.com/paradigm> (14 February 2018)

[10] The concept of paradigm shift is associated with the debate on the development of scientific knowledge. Thomas Kuhn, who has contributed a great deal to this debate, points out that a paradigm gives direction and a time of reference for intellectual activity at a given time. It should, however, be noted that a changeover from one paradigm to another is never smooth in the intellectual community. Newer paradigms are accepted with a great deal of hesitation and questioning by a community of researchers, with the result that sometimes more than one paradigm exists simultaneously. David J. Bosch, *Transforming Mission: Paradigm shifts in Theology of Mission* (New York: Orbis Books, 1991), 182-183.

[11] Bosch, *Transforming Mission*, 181-182.

[12] *Modality* and *Sodality* are terms used by Ralph Winter to explain structures that were evolved by the Church to carry on God's redemptive mission in the world in response to new situations and challenges. 'Modality' refers to the local church. 'Sodality' refers to mission structures such as the missionary orders, monasteries or nunneries, organizations, fellowships, or missionary bands. These two structures have continuously appeared across the centuries. Mission efforts will be most effective only if both of these two structures are fully and properly involved and supportive of each other. Ralph Winter, "The Two Structures of God's Redemptive Mission," in *Perspectives on the World Christian Movement: A Reader* (Fourth Edition) (eds. Ralph Winter and Steven C. Hawthorne; California: William Carey Library, 2009), 245.

[13] Bosch, *Transforming Mission*, xv, 511, 353.

[14] Bosch, *Transforming Mission*, 354.

[15] Bosch, *Transforming Mission*, 355.

[16] Las G. Newman in *Holistic Mission: God's Plan for God's People* (eds. Brian Woolnough and Wonsuk Ma, *Holistic Mission*, ix.<https://digitalshowcase.oru.edu/cgi/viewcontent.cgi?article=1010&context=re2010series> (14 February 2018)

[17] It was at the Wheaton '83 Conference that the issue of "Gospel in the context of human need" was raised, and there it was proposed that the purpose of the Gospel is nothing less than total social transformation. David Bosch, who was present at Wheaton '83, then wrote *Transforming Mission* where he traces the paradigm shifts in mission theology. Siga Arles, "'Transforming World' A Call of Our Times: Content, Context and Convergence," in *Contemporary Issues Booklet No. 1*, (eds. Siga Arles and Peter S. C. Pothan; Bangalore: Centre for Contemporary Christianity, 2010), 2-3

[18] Bosch, *Transforming Mission*, 390-391.

[19] Bosch, *Transforming Mission*, 9-11.

[20] Masilamani Azariah, *Dream and Reality: CSI after 60 Years* (Chennai: CSI Diocese of Madras, 2007), 17.

[21] David Selvaraj, "Transformation – An Ongoing Agenda for Mission" in *Church of South India Synod, Priorities for the Mission of the Church for the Decade 2011 – 2020* (Chennai: Church of South India, 2010), 31-32.

[22] K. C. Abraham, "The Church of South India in the Twenty-First Century: Ministry and Mission," in *United to Unite: History of the Church of South India, 1947-1997* (ed. J. W. Gladstone; Chennai: Oxford University-Press, 1997), 154.

## Bibliography

Abraham, K. C. "The Church of South India in the Twenty-First Century: Ministry and Mission." Page 154 in *United to Unite: History of the Church of South India, 1947-1997*. Edited by J. W. Gladstone. Chennai: Oxford University-Press, 1997.

Arles, Siga. "'Transforming World' A Call of Our Times: Content, Context and Convergence," Pages 390-391 in *Contemporary Issues Booklet No. 1*. Edited by Siga Arles and Peter S. C. Pothan. Bangalore: Centre for Contemporary Christianity, 2010.

Azariah, Masilamani. *Dream and Reality: CSI after 60 Years*. Chennai: CSI Diocese of Madras, 2007.

Bosch, David J. *Transforming Mission: Paradigm shifts in Theology of Mission*. New York: Orbis Books, 1991.

Chandran, J. R., ed. *The Joint Council of CSI – CNI – MTC – A Brief History and Interpretation.* Delhi: ISPCK, 1984.

Hollis, Michael. *The Significance of South India.* London: Lutterworth,1966.

Paul, Rajaiah D. *The First Decade: An Account of the Church of South India.* Madras: Christian Literature Society, 1958.

Selvaraj, David. "Transformation – An Ongoing Agenda for Mission." Pages 31-32 in *Church of South India Synod, Priorities for the Mission of the Church for the Decade 2011 – 2020.* Chennai: Church of South India, 2010.

Winter, Ralph. "The Two Structures of God's Redemptive Mission." Page 245 in *Perspectives on the World Christian Movement: A Reader.* Edited by Ralph Winter and Steven C. Hawthorne. California: William Carey Library, 2009.

*CSI Life,* Magazine of the Church of South India, Supplementary Issue, October 2017, Volume XV/Issue 10a, 127.

CSI Synod, "History of Church of South India." <http://www.csisynod.com/> (14 October 2012).

CSI Synod, "History of Church of South India." <http://www.csisynod.com/> (14 October 2012).

2

# A Mission Reading of the Concept of Life in Ezekiel 37: 1-14 & Mark 1:29–39

**Rebecca Azariah**

Today the mission of the Church to the world is being realized in a new way. We live in a world that is unique, complicated, and dynamic. The world is shaped by multiculturalism and pluralism, marked with global realities of migration, urbanization and globalization leading to deep transformations in the political, cultural and economic situation of all nations. The mission of the Church is rooted amidst all these developments and a society that is marked by distrust, alienation and violence. The church ought to be interculturally[1] competent, developing relational skills to bridge and build authentic relationships. "Fullness of life" is the message of our Lord and Saviour Jesus Christ. This life has been distorted and has not been able to reach its fullness. Mission is to invite people to this fullness of life that is to help the suffering and struggling people to realize that they are the children of God who is the life-giver, life sustainer and life fulfiller. He is the creator of all people groups including the women irrespective of culture, religion, politics, ideology, caste and faith. According to David Bosch Mission is to restore their life and dignity to the fullness so that the image of God may be realized among them.[2]

Jesus Christ came so that all may have abundant life. He liberates the oppressed people, establishes justice, overthrowing the structures of all kinds of oppression. He works among the suffering people in the establishment of God's sovereign rule of justice. It is *oikonomia* of God in which people may be socio-economically secure for the fullness of their life and enjoy a free and secure culturally abundant and secure life in the society.[3]

This paper attempts to do a mission reading of the concept of life. The biblical texts selected for the study are Ezekiel 37: 1–14 and Mark 1:29–39

## Meaning of Mission

"The word mission comes from the Latin word *mittere*, which means "to send." It is the equivalent of the Greek word *apostello*, which also means "to send.". "Mission" carries a holistic understanding: the proclamation and sharing of the good news of the gospel by word *(kerygma)*, deed (*diakonia*), prayer and worship (*liturgia*) and the everyday witness of the Christian life *(martyria)*; teaching as building up and strengthening people in their relationship with God and each other; and healing as wholeness and reconciliation into *koinonia* — communion with God, communion with people, and communion with creation as a whole.[4] The mission of God (*Missio Dei*) has no limits or barriers; it has been addressed to and has been at work within the entire human race and the whole of creation throughout history. Mission is God's mission in which Christians are mere participants in the process of witnessing, proclamation, worship, inculturation, and contextualization in the world. The church is sent out to the world, empowered by the Holy Spirit, announcing the Gospel of Jesus Christ[5] in word and deed, witnessing to the kingdom of God.[6] Thus the church is a healing and caring community for all humanity in the world, standing in solidarity with the oppressed, downtrodden, and marginalized and participating in the process of liberation from the various bondages and bringing in transformation. Therefore mission is God's gift and a compelling responsibility from God. It means as in the prayer of St. Francis of Assisi, 'being instruments of peace' in this world.

Borderless church and Christian mission refer to the people chosen and called by God to participate in God's mission that is to build the kingdom of God inclusive of all humanity and creation. In Rev 7:9–10, John gives us a glimpse of the Borderless Church, he describes a great multitude from every nation, tribe, people and language standing before the throne and in front of the Lamb singing his praises. Ecclesia is the church, the called out people empowered by the power of the Triune God to be the transformative community resisting the evil structures in society and being a life-giving and life-affirming community to all people irrespective of caste, creed, gender, religion, and education. The motive of the mission of the church is to invite people to realize that they are the children of God

## Meaning of Life

Life is inherited by all creation. Webster's definition of life is "the sequence of physical and mental experiences that make up the existence of an individual." "Indeed life is a continuum of accomplishment, failure, discovery, dilemma, challenge, boredom, sadness, disappointment, appreciation, the giving and receipt of grace, empathy, peace, and our reactions to all sorts of stimuli- love, touch, friendship, loss."[7] This life is given through Christ to be nurtured among all people and all creation. Therefore life is to pursue being human in all his/her fullness and flourishing through communication, understanding and service.[8] Everyone has a story, life cannot be planned, and there is failure, disappointments, joys, and happy surprises. [9] Life can be full only when we communicate. We are not isolated creatures; we live as part of the culture, people groups, science and technology. In order to communicate we have to understand the world and oneself in the world. We need to understand the friends and the enemies of life. The friends promote life while enemies distort the meaning of life. When the enemies are analysed and understood only then one can be involved in improving oneself through service to humankind which can help oneself and others to live life in all its fullness. Today there are many obstacles such as lack of friendship, neighbourliness, good media, and a nourishing culture. All of which hinders oneself and others from having a meaningful life.[10]

## Distortion of Life in Different Contexts

On September 1, 2017 the state of Tamil Nadu in India was shocked and filled with sorrow, tears, and confusion when S. Anitha,[11] a 17 year old, extremely bright student scoring 1176 marks out 1200 in her standard 12 Board exams and a MBBS aspirant, committed suicide after discovering that she could not pursue her dream of becoming a doctor due to the introduction of NEET[12] exams. She was completely disillusioned and disappointed. The life of Anitha was distorted by the NEET exams.

According to the Cambridge Dictionary the word "distort" means "to change something from its usual, original, natural or intended meaning, condition or shape". Life can be distorted in varied ways, in this paper a reading is made from Mark 1:29–34 and Ezekiel 37:1–14 to see the varied ways this could happen. Some of the contexts in Mark which can be read through these passages where life can be distorted are analysed one by one below.

## *"Now Simon's Mother-in-law was in Bed with Fever…." (Mk 1:29)*

"Simon's mother-in-law was in bed with a fever". Which literally means that she is in bed, flat on her back, did not have energy or enthusiasm because she was separated from family, friends, and her usual activities. She could not live her life to the fullness, something had distorted her life. Her world was small, confined to that of her bed. She is confined to a horizontal existence. The fever could be related to the evil structures of the society which makes us confined to ourselves unable to enjoy the life which Jesus intends for us. It leaves us horizontal and disconnected from the source and origin of life; disconnected from love, joy, forgiveness, beauty, justice, mercy, compassion, generosity, wisdom, and all the other divine attributes that give meaning to our lives, content to our relationships, and direction and purpose to what we do.

I will deal with two of the many social evils in the Indian context which I feel are the root causes of the different challenges that India faces today. The two "Fever States" that can be identified in the Indian context are: Caste and Gender inequality. The caste system is a system that defines class[13] or assigns status to individuals by virtue of birth.[14] This confines the humans to a particular self and to communities that promote inequality, undemocratic nature, feelings of superiority and inferiority and an increased gap between upper and lower caste people. Gender Inequality is discrimination between men and women. In the Indian context men are considered far superior to women in all fields. Women have been thought to take care of home and family while men are to protect and earn a livelihood for the family. Although in the recent past this situation has changed there are still several discriminatory practices practiced against women in the society such as violence, harassment and exploitation. These lead to various challenges in society. Some of the challenges are as follows: Dowry system where the parents pay huge money to the boy's family when their daughter gets married. This leads to a non-preference for a girl child as parents want to avoid the dowry burden and hence opt for abortions of female foetuses, thus distorting the life of the baby girl even in the womb. The dowry practice also leads to female Infanticide which is the most shameful social evil in India. It also leads to violence against women which can be categorized into several broad categories. These include violence carried out by "individuals" as well as "states". Some of the forms of violence perpetrated by individuals are rape, domestic violence, sexual harassment, female infanticide, as well as harmful traditional practices such as honour killings, dowry violence, and female genital mutilation, marriage by abduction and forced marriage. Other forms are such as mob violence and trafficking of the women and force them to prostitution are societal evils that are caused by the social structures. Poverty is another area where life has been disturbed. Poverty is the absolute deprivation of basic needs which include food, water, shelter and money. This has given rise to various other problems such as unemployment, child labour, child exploitation and prostitution. All these are "fever states" that shape the lives of people differently., They are confined to themselves just as Simon's mother-in-law was confined to the bed, not able to move, disconnected with the people so also these issues cripple the people so that they are no longer the same; some of them live with feelings of hurt, shame, remorse, guilt, discouragement and distress. They have no hope.

### *"....Set me down in the midst of the valley; and it was full of bones...and indeed they were dry." (Ezekiel 37:1–2)*

God had called his people, the Jews, out of captivity in Egypt. For over 100 years they had been in Egyptian captivity. God brought them into the promised land, and gave them a land and a king, and made them a nation. But they turned against God and God allowed them to go into captivity once again. Nebuchadnezzar and his Babylonian army invaded Israel. They had reduced Solomon's Temple to ashes, and had taken many of the Jewish people back to Babylon as captives. This is the condition that the people of Israel and the prophet Ezekiel were in. The nation of Israel is dead. But God has a vision for Ezekiel in chapter 37:1–2 – Ezekiel is carried to a valley full of very dry bones. These bones are scattered everywhere, very white and very dry. Bones all over the place scattered by the wild animals so that there is nothing but miscellaneous bones as far as the eyes can see. The peace of this eerie solitude that had been rudely broken by the shrieks of the wounded, the wild shouts of the victors, the clash of the arms and the savage roar of war, was silent and calm now. The storm was down and the tempest that swept over it had left it strewn with wrecks.[15]

At present India also is dead with all its corruption, evil structures, unfaithful and greedy political leaders. The uncertain world is filled with suffering, oppression and death.[16] We live in a peaceless world. The lives of women in many parts of India are gripped with the cold grip of death rather than freedom of life. Violence against women includes domestic[17], State[18] and Social[19] violence - all these demonic distortion of human values continue to destroy God's world and his people. Economic exploitation and economic injustice dominate the relationship between the rich and the poor. Racism, inequality and casteism are all sanctified by the law itself. Our world is groaning and there is no longer the joyful, hopeful sound heard but it is the sound of gunfire, children screaming and voice of the powerless…[20]

In the midst of the ghastly skeletons where there is neither a sign nor a sound of life, Ezekiel stands charged with the strange question "….can these bones live"? Is there life in these white and dry unsepulchered corpses wintered by the birds and the wild beasts, washed and bleached by the sun and rain[21]. The hope is totally cut off. In India in many places women and children die of hunger; people who stand for justice and human rights are killed. There are many young people whose future has been distorted and their life is powdered to dust by the threat of coming systems in the world.[22] S. Anitha committed suicide because of the NEET exams. Young children in India are being tortured in the schools, beaten and slapped by teachers; they are even being molested and raped. "Can these bones live? Is there hope in such situations where life is distorted? Every act of inhumanity, every unjust law, every justification of violence and oppression is a distortion and denial of life which God bestows on his people.

## *Life in its Fullness as the Missio Dei*

Abundant life is a term used to refer to Christian teachings on fullness of life. This may include expectations of prosperity and health but may also include other forms of fullness of life when faced with adverse circumstances.[23] The Federation of Asian Bishops Conferences in its Fifth Plenary Assembly held at Bandung, Indonesia, in 1990, states an integral understanding of mission… "Mission being a continuation in the spirit of mission of Christ, involves a being with the people, as was Jesus: 'The word became flesh and dwelt among us' (Jn 1:14). Therefore, mission includes: being with the people, responding to their needs, with sensitiveness to the presence of God in cultures and other religious traditions, and witnessing to the values of God's kingdom through dialogue with Asia's poor[24], with its local culture, and other religious traditions."[25] The fullness of life for a person begins with a new birth, a new relationship with God, new motivations, and a new relationship with humankind.[26] Abundant life teaches prosperity and health for the total human being, including the body, mind, emotions, relationships, material needs, and eternal life.[27] It also includes physical and material prosperity and good health and wellbeing.

A few insights of fullness of life as the Missio Dei that we can derive from the two texts are outlined below:

### *Mission as Life-Giving (Mark 1:30–31 and Ezekiel 37:1,2)*

Jesus "took her by the hand and lifted her up" (Mark 1:30) means that God gives life to the sick woman. She was no longer confined to a horizontal existence. She stood upright. Jesus broke her fever and restored her vertical connection. With that restoration all the other connections of her life were renewed. Jesus "lifted her up" is about more than just changing positions. It's more than just getting out of bed. This woman has been healed, made whole, and raised to new life. In Ezekiel 37: 1, 2 which talks about life given to the lifeless, the bones were dry. They were in a hopeless situation. India's search is characterized by the self-contradictions of the socio-political system created and its apparent failure to translate the vision of the fullness of life into reality for a majority of the people. The atrocities on the weaker sections of people, caste violence, the traumatic experiences of women victims of rape are an insult to our human dignity.[28] The

Bible testifies that God is the one who chooses people in the margins which include women (Exod 3). Blessed are the poor for they shall inherit the kingdom of God (Matt 5). It is among the oppressed, impure and excluded people in Egypt, Babylon, and Nazareth that God revealed himself as the liberator, compassionate mother and father.[29] Jesus restores the woman. The fever left her and she started to serve him. Envisioning Christian mission among women who are one among the marginalized people is not only binding the wounds of the victims or offering actions of compassion but it calls us to confront and transform the forces which cause suffering and deprivation.[30] Some of the burning issues have been neglected. The bones in the graveyard also were neglected; whoever went to such a place don't give importance to the bones; it is even more surprising when God tells Ezekiel to speak to the dry bones in 37:4, and he begins to preach to these dead, dry bones, and says, "Dry bones, listen to what God has to say." In the word of God, there is life and it is an abundant life. Through the word of God impelled by the spirit of faith and love, we ought to raise and recover the fallen humanity.[31] As we learn God's wisdom we should also be in God's work. We ought to be in solidarity with the people denied life and help them through God to have an abundant life. Mission involves dismantling oppressive systems such as patriarchy, racism, casteism and other discriminatory and exclusionary practices[32] that create the world of oppression, discrimination and inequality, which confine women and do not allow her to enjoy the abundant life which Jesus intends for her.

## *Mission as Transformed Life (Mark 1:31 and Ezekiel 37:8–9)*

The life that we see in these two passages is that when the word of God is proclaimed there is a transformation. When Ezekiel starts to preach… something begins to happen… right before his eyes (37:7–8). The bones came together – muscle and flesh and skin began to surround the skeletons. The bones which had no life now were beautifully transforming. As human beings in his mission, we collaborate with

God in bringing his original designs in creation to historical perfection. God's plan for his people is multifaceted.[33] Through our proclamation and actions, our efforts should be continuous in restoring life wherever there are distortions. It is not enough only to proclaim, we should also be involved in action as we see in Mark 1:30-31: "He came and took her by the hand and lifted her up. Then the fever left her." Jesus by his transforming touch helps the woman to stand again. The touch of Jesus transforms all evils in the society; in hopeless situations it gives hope. This is what missionaries like William Carey, Bartholomew Ziegenbalg, and many others did. Through their lives they manifested the love of God and brought many transformations in society. Our mission involves being in a genuine struggle as God involves in the struggle of the defenseless people. *Missio Dei* means participation in God's mission. It is participating in the divine act of liberation that we resist the dominant system that obstructs any individual towards the restoration of the *imago Dei*. This invites us to be advocates of human rights and upholders of human worth.[34] In a world where the poor, women and other marginalized has no value, it is a challenge to be the voice of these people and transform their lives in helping them live a life of dignity, rights and worth.

### *Mission as Spirit Filled Life (Ezekiel 37: 14)*

"I will put My Spirit in you, and you shall live, and I will place you in your own land. Then you shall know that I, the Lord, have spoken it and performed it," says the Lord.

This Spirit Filled life has three dimensions:

### i. Spirit of Truth

The Spirit which God breathed into the dry bones was a Spirit of Truth. In order that Christ may come in the unclean things ought to go, if we love God, the truth is within us, and the truth sets us free casts out all errors and helps us to be witnesses as children of God[35]. In the present, there are many embittered and hate relationships in the society because of the many truths. Human solidarity is distorted into sub-identities and loyalties, the dominant features in society are caste division, gender division, class division, hatred based on competitive ambition and selfish desires is destroying the harmony, peace and unity in the society which in turn affects the lives of the people. Through the Spirit of Truth, we need to de-mask[36] and demystify[37] the powers of injustice, oppression, discrimination and other evil powers and bring the message of truth which sets us free through the words of healing and promise.

### ii. Spirit of Love

The Spirit which God breathed into the dry bones was a Spirit of Love. God is Spirit (Jn 4:24) defines God according to his work in the world and God is love (1 John 4:8) describes God's mode of action and working. It refers to how God miraculously and wonderfully deals with humankind out of his spirit and in his love.[38] God's love restores people. What Ezek 37:14 means is that God says I shall place you in your own land; settle you there in peace and quietness, in safety and security and in the enjoyment of all mercies and privileges, temporal and spiritual: this is the love of God. *Missio Dei* is the mission of God where God is the initiator of missions. He is the fountain of love. The world is like a valley of dry bones, ugly in its wickedness, helpless in its confusion, utterly unable to save itself.[39] God's love crosses boundaries; he is in solidarity with the ones in the margins, the rejected.[40] God in and through his love gave life to the most degraded, desolate and despairing condition[41] of humankind. God's love involves reaching out through acts of compassionate justice to include those marginalized and excluded by society. [42]

### iii. Spirit of Life

This account is a figurative description of God's creation of a new Israel. Even though that new creation begins with the remains of the old Israel, the exiles under the image of dry bones, depicting a totally hopeless situation, the new Israel is radically different: it is an ideal people, shaped by God's spirit to live the covenant faithfully. Ezekiel 37: 14 "then shall ye know that I the Lord have spoken it, and performed it, says the Lord;" implies that all this was his promise, foretold by him, notified to them by his prophets, and now fully accomplished; which they would observe with wonder and thankfulness, and give him the glory of it. The life we live or which has been given by God is rooted in him (Rom 8: 9-11). He dwells in us and his power works from within manifesting in word and deed. The life filled with the Spirit is actively evident in bearing the fruits that are found in Gal 5:22-23: "But the fruit of the Spirit is love, joy, peace, longsuffering, kindness, goodness, faithfulness, gentleness, self-control…." Therefore as we participate in the mission of God we ought to remain true to the Spirit and the message of the Gospel of Jesus. He brought life to sinners, women, outcastes and the poor. Our mission should bring the *imago Dei* that is dignified and full life for every human being as God intends. It should enable people to move towards the fullness of life in Christ.

## Conclusion

We live in a post-truth era filled with alternative facts. Our mission field, is troubled by great adversity and many of us who are just starting out are wondering, "Can these Bones Live?" How do we deal with these dry bones, dead situations, bleached and bleak realities? Jesus was committed to a mission that is to give life in fullness to all created beings. Ezekiel the prophet is asked to preach to the dry bones which are cold, dead and utterly indifferent. Just as Jesus gave his hand to Simon Peter's mother-in-law and the fever left her so also when Ezekiel started to preach the word of God an awful scene is witnessed and the bones shake and move and fit themselves together with flesh, sinews and skin to cover them. So also our mission is involved with a despairing world where our frustrations find expressions as found in Ezekiel 37:11: "… our bones are dried as living beings we are dead;

our hope is lost…". We don't have hope as to whether we will have an abundant life; and we are cut off from our parts; we don't have a part in the land of the living, we are lost. Ezekiel's preaching and Jesus' healing touch brought life so also our deeds and words should bring the life that God intended for the world. Let us rediscover mission methods and strategies in order to be fully involved in concentrating on the manifestation of the kingdom of God in its fullness especially to the ones who are victimized by the various evils in the society. Let us be involved in the mission of unity and be united in our lives to value, support, uplift, affirm, and encourage humans, let our deeds and words advocate for women and the marginalized; encouraging them to self-acceptance and emotional wellbeing.

## Endnotes

[1] Communication of God's love in different cultures following the principles of inculturation.

[2] David Bosch, *Transforming Mission: Paradigm Shifts in Theology of Mission* (New York: Orbis Books, 1991), 331.

[3] David Bosch, *Transforming Mission,* 331.

[4] WCC Conference On World Mission And Evangelism *Come, Holy Spirit- Heal And Reconcile; Called In Christ To Be Reconciling And Healing Communities* (Greece, Athens) 12-19 May 2005.

[5] The Gospel is the Good News. The Good news of abundant life, transformation, liberation and reconciliation

[6] The purpose of Mission is the Kingdom of God. The church is a means to achieve it through its witness. Dr. K.C.Abraham says Witness is the expression of God's love for humanity for which Christians are to be the effective tools. It involves the right relationship with God, humanity and the world at large. It involves loving one's neighbour as oneself and engaging in such activities in the society for the glory of God.

[7] "What is Life" in *Philosophy of Life: A Magazine of Ideas,* <https://philosophynow.org/issues/101/What_Is_Life> (25 May 2018)

[8] < https://www.theschooloflife.com/thebookoflife/category/self-knowledge/know-yourself/> (25 May 2018)

[9] What is Life" in *Philosophy of Life: A Magazine of Ideas,* <https://philosophynow.org/issues/101/What_Is_Life> (25 May 2018)

[10] "What is Life" in *Philosophy of Life: A Magazine of Ideas,* <https://philosophynow.org/issues/101/What_Is_Life> (25 May 2018)

[11] S. Anitha was from the village called Sendurai in the most backward district of Ariyalur in Tamil Nadu. She was the daughter of a Dalit daily wage labourer.

[12] National Eligibility and Entrance Test

[13] Four Classes include 1. The Brahmins – Priestly class 2. The Kshatriyas – Warriors and ruler class 3. The Vaishyas – Traders and 4. Sudras – Domestic servants and laborers

[14] <http://www.importantindia.com/17493/social-issues-in-india> (March 23,2015)

[15] George, Barlow, *The Preacher's Complete Homiletic Commentary on Ezekiel* (Michigan: Baker's Books; 1996) 397.

[16] David Gill, *Gathered For Life* (Geneva: WCC Publications,1983) 222.

[17] Domestic Violence refers to violence between spouses. It can also refer to the exploitation which woman face from the landlord, mistress or master of the homes they go to work where they are treated badly, have no holidays, are sexually abused, misguided, abducted and even sold.

[18] The State discriminates women in the name of population control. Pinto in his book *Violence on Women and the Need for non-formal Education,* Vol 4.; 17-19, says "women are treated as guinea pigs …"; Horrible crimes area done on women. The so called development programmes have often disintegrated family life especially among rural and tribal women who have ended up in prostitution.

[19] In rural areas and among tribal populations women are branded as witches; Widows have no support in the society and are mistreated.

[20] David Gill, *Gathered For Life* 223.

[21] George Barlow, *The Preacher's Complete Homiletic,* 397.

[22] David Gill, *Gathered For Life* 223

[23] John 10:10

[24] Poor includes women who are victimized , marginalized, traumatized in the society.

[25] Rosales. B.G. and Arevalo, C.G. (ed)., *For all the Peoples of Asia, Federation of Asian Bishops' Conferences, Documents from 1970-1991*, (Philippines: Claretian Publishers, 1992) 280.

[26] Fritz Ridenour, *So What's the Difference?* (California: Regal Books, 1967) 97, 107.

[27] The study notes on John 10: 10 from "The Spirit Filled Life Bible" <https://web.archive.org/web/20091214063756/http:/www.livingway.org/library/faq/faq001.htm> (25 May 2018)

[28] Joseph Velamkunnel, "Mission as Liberation" in *Dimensions of Mission in India* (ed. Joseph Mattam and Sebastian Kim; Bombay: St Paul Press, 1995). 87.

[29] Mohan Larbeer P, *Re-Location of Mission and Ecumenism in the context of Margins* (Bangalore: BTESSC, 2014) 39.

[30] Mohan Larbeer P, *Re-Location of Mission* 42.

[31] George Barlow, *The Preacher's Complete Homiletic,* 399.

[32] George Barlow, *The Preacher's Complete Homiletic,* 399.

[33] George Barlow, *The Preacher's Complete Homiletic,* 88

[34] Mohan Larbeer P, *Re-Location of Mission,* 49.

[35] George Barlow, *The Preacher's Complete Homiletic,* 408.

[36] Samuel W. Meshack, Eberhard Von De Heyde., eds., *Communication of the Gospel in the context of Globalisation, Religious Pluralism and Nationalism* (Chennai: GLTC, 2002), 128.

[37] Samuel W. Meshack, *Communication of the Gospel,* 128.

[38] George R. Beasley-Murray, "John",*Word Biblical Commentary* (Texas: Words Books Publishers, 1987), 62.

[39] H.D.M. Spence and Joseph S. Exell., "Ezekiel" *The Pulpit Commentary* (Massachusetts:Hendrickson Publishers, ...) 269.

[40] Mohan Larbeer P, *Re-Location of Mission,* 48-49.

[41] Mohan Larbeer P, *Re-Location of Mission* 269.

[42] Paul D. Hanson, "Isaiah 40-66", *Interpretation: A Bible Commentary for Teaching and Preaching* (Louisville: Westminster John Knox Press, 1995) 204-205.

## Bibliography

Barlow, George. *The Preacher's Complete Homiletic Commentary on Ezekiel.* Michigan: Baker's Books, 1996.

Beasley-Murray, George R. "John", in Word *Biblical Commentary.* Texas: Words Books Publishers, 1987.

Bosch, David. *Transforming Mission: Paradigm Shifts in Theology of Mission.* New York: Orbis Books, 1991.

Gill, David. *Gathered For Life.* Geneva: WCC Publications, 1983.

Larbeer P, Mohan. *Re-Location of Mission and Ecumenism in the context of Margins*. Bangalore: BTESSC, 2014.

Meshack, Samuel W. and Eberhard Von De Heyde., eds., *Communication of the Gospel in the context of Globalisation, Religious Pluralism and Nationalism*. Chennai: GLTC, 2002.

Ridenour, Fritz. *So What's the Difference?* California: Regal Books, 1967.

Rosales, B.G. and Arevalo, C.G. (ed)., *For all the Peoples of Asia, Federation of Asian Bishops' Conferences, Documents from 1970-1991*. Philippines: Claretian Publishers, 1992.

Spence, H.D.M. and Joseph S. Exell., "Ezekiel" in *The Pulpit Commentary. Massachusetts*: Hendrickson Publishers, 1985.

Velamkunnel, Joseph. "Mission as Liberation." in *Dimensions of Mission in India*. Edited by Joseph Mattam and Sebastian Kim. Bombay: St Paul Press, 1995.

3

# Zionist Conversation and Conversion Path of Prophetic Diakonia

**Praveen P.S. Perumalla**

The CSI on its commemoration of 70 years of life and ministries envisions a "Borderless Ecclesia." In this paper I delve into this theme of "Borderless Ecclesia" affirming prophetic Diakonia.

Any decisive move towards borderless in a prophetic tradition is a deliberate move out of the closed cage of religion, which is otherwise perceived as private and personal. Even God is perceived to exist in order to fulfill private and personal prosperity. To move out of such enclosures and conceptually constructed borders it is imperative to touch upon the core political issues that affect the lives of people and nations. Such a move can be understood as the Christian faith calling for deeper commitment towards non-members (of Church) and environment in affirmation of fullness of life.

CSI needs to be perceived as belonging to Asia, and leading the way forward toward borderless ecclesia. An important dimension of Asian realities is increasing poverty, emigration and refugee crisis, violence on communities and nature. The Middle-Eastern has been experiencing emigration and refugee crisis on the one hand and State building through static border lines on the other. Commenting on the static perception of border lines, a well-known social anthropologist Thomas Fedrick Weybye Barth, popularly known as Fedrick Barth, says "... boundary lines... (sets) limits that mark social groups off from each other and finally ... that which separates distinct categories of the mind."[1] Two important aspects are highlighted by Barth, the physical and abstract aspects of boundary lines. There are physical disturbances to a given topography, eco-system, and there are abstract aspects of communities that are segregated. Some abstract aspects are the spirit of rejection, hatred towards the other induced in them. Such boundary lines signify a constructed "other one," an exclusionary category. The political meaning of the "other one" creates a new category called "stateless people." Commenting on the political meaning of the "other one" from Israel-Palestine experiences, it is said,

> Palestinian emigration can be considered as a byproduct of the creation of the state of Israel and the absence of a Palestinian state. Palestinian identity, like the Kurdish one, is not represented in the region by a territorially based state, delimited by international borders. Exile, statelessness and refugeeness are then some of the results of state building in the region. [2]

But, the overall experiences of Asian and African countries since 1940's and 50's is different to that of the Israel - Palestine experience of forcefully erecting boundary walls. The newly independent nations in Asia and Africa chose a political path of "non-aligned movement" and presented themselves to the rest of the world at the "the Bandung Conference" (1955). The vision was to build Asia and Africa without any borders namely racism, colonialism, and imperialism; free from every form of dependency syndrome that leads to slavery. The focus was on the political dismantling of border building powers in affirmation of democracy and freedom.

A premature stage of Asio-African political movement had pushed the nations of both continents into a crisis of emigration and colonialism of different kinds. To answer the spirit of Asio-Africa that longs for freedom from strong borders of racism, casteism, colonialism, imperialism, and hatred towards others, the dire need is an awakened civil society that takes active role in political and legal activism in order to realize borderless spaces. Such an effort necessitates borders or boundary lines of every nation-state to be conceptualised as non-static dynamic spaces that address human concerns at large.

This paper reflects upon "political Zionism" to understand borders or boundary lines. At the same time, prophetic diakonia with the vision of borderless ecclesia is explored to some extent in response to the ongoing bordering as Asian realities.

## Political Zionism

To some extent Indians seems to be familiar with Hindutva and the Sangh Parivar, but we are not very familiar with political Zionism. This paper reflects upon political Zionism that has been influencing contemporary geo-politics of the world, centred on the Middle- East. Political Zionism is influencing Indian politics, Indian Church and is something Indian Church cannot afford to ignore while choosing to be a borderless ecclesia.

Some salient aspects of political Zionism are delineated here in brief. 1). Political Zionism is an ideology, whose origin runs parallel to the origin of New European Nationalism of boundary segregation characterized by racist hostility and anti-Semitism.[3] 2). Political Zionism has been translating into a project of establishing a Jewish State nurtured by Jewish nationalism.[4] 3). Towards the idea of forming a Jewish State, the word "Zion" (1890) was manipulated to carry political meaning by Theodore Herzl[5] to raise funds for the Jewish nation for purchase of landed property exclusively for Jews, creation of Jewish agricultural villages, and *Aliyah* (immigration of Jews) to occupy Palestine.[6] 4) The preferred settlement of Jews, as far as the Zionist lobby is concerned, is in the land of Palestine. Moreover, Herzl's interest in forming a Jewish State intends to model the modern monarch, the

German Kaiser.[7] Philipp of Eulenburg, Kaiser's best friend thought of Zionism as a way to extend German power.[8] French (Napoleon) and Britain are said to be competing in order to become champions over Palestine and both are said to be interested in restraining Russia and expanding powers up to India thus strategically controlling Palestine.[9] 5). In spite of many strategies by Political Zionists strong opposition to the ideolgy of political Zionism has been expressed from different sectors namely Orthodox Jews, Internationalists and others. The

Orthodox Jewish understanding of "Zionism" is religious, reminiscent of Messaianic expectations and has nothing to do with *Aliyah* (immigration of Jews) to Palestine. Their fears associated with political Zionism are reflected in strong opposition to *Aliyah* thus paving way for the eruption of racist anti-Semitism.[10] The internationalists who struggled against Tsarist regime (Emperor Nicholas II) in Russia also hold a similar opinion to that of the Orthodox Jews on the potency of political Zionism to give birth to racist anti-Semitism in Asia.[11]

In spite of the exclusivist politics of political Zionism, the idea of Socialist Zionism is also prevalent. This view is represented by Ben-Gurion, who is said to be instrumental in creating *kibbutz* – a collective formed, hoping that Jews will live and work together in agriculture with the rest of the population in Palestine.[12] The idea of keeping Holy places outside of any form of political control is also part of the socialist conception of forming a new State in Palestine: "Herzl later decided that Jerusalem should be shared: We shall extra-territorialize Jerusalem so that it will belong to nobody and everybody, its Holy Places the joint possession of all Believers." [13]

In the next sections I discuss two variables namely "Zionist Conversation" and "Conversion to Zionism".

## Zionist Conversation

"Science and Zionism overlapped…."[14]

To realize the project of "political Zionism" i.e. to form a Jewish State in the land of Palestine, is a difficult task as it has to deal with "anti-Semitism" and alternative views prevalent among the rulers of the West, even among the Jews in the West. Herezl is said to be the first person to present the idea of political Zionism which was not welcomed either by the French or the British. In spite of this strong rejection on many fronts incessant persuasion by the Political Zionists starting from Herzl to Ben-Gurion and others made it come true. In short, it was the winning over of anti-Semitism and the opposition to the alternative settlement of Jews.[15] In order to win over the powerful rulers of the West as well as win consensus of majority of the Jewish Orthodox, "Zionist Conversation" is an important instrument. Zionist Conversation can be said to be "…not built from the bottom by settlers but, granted by emperors and financed by plutocrats."[16]

In this paper the word "Zionist Conversation" is used to convey the idea of colonial interests prioritised over other progressive approaches. Zionist Conversation employs several strategies. Firstly the colonial war context on the one hand and scientific discoveries on the other complement each other and are instrumentalised in fulfilling the Political Zionist project. Secondly lobbying for the Zionist project is carried out including the use of media namely *Manchester Guardian* through the writing of Dr. Chaim Weizmann, CP Scott and others. Thirdly persuading colonial powers to move away from the "poisonous hydra of Jewish Capitalism"[17]and from being anti-Semitic.

In the context of the first world war, Winston Churchill wanted more bombs, therefore more of acetone solvent. He called Dr. Chaim Weizmann, a Russian-born scientist in the field of chemistry, who studied science in Germany and Switzerland and embraced political Zionism from his childhood. Weizmann was asked to make 30,000 tons of acetone solvent and he gladly obliged to the request of Churchill as

Weizmann had discovered a new formula to manufacture acetone.[18] Weizmann could fulfill the war requirements of the colonial British. He thus entered into Zionist Conversation with the British authorities negotiating for a Jewish State. Some of the prominent non-Jews who had earlier held views negating a Jewish State surprised Dr. Weizmann by declaring themselves Zionists. They are Winston Churchill, Lloyd George, Author Balfour[19] and others.

The Zionist conversations are said to be persuading the Jewish people across Europe, particularly in Great Britain, as well as to British Statesmen. The instrument applied in Zionist Conversation is the national newspaper *Manchester Guardian* and notably some of its staff namely Harry Sacher, CP Scott, others, and Herbert Sidebotham a British imperialist.

The British colonial powers changed their mind-set in the interest of colonial expansion and control of the region including the need for American support in war[20] and consented to support the Political Zionist project. Further at least 34 different plans were proposed to locate Jews either in Africa or Asia.[21] But, Zionist Conversation was politically designed in such a manner that the colonial powers ultimately agreed to give Palestine for Jewish State.

Prior to the political Zionism project, it is said that different communities were moving into the land of Palestine[22] and there were communities already living in the land like Persians, Yemenites, Palestinian Christians/ Arab Christians, Armenian Christians, Palestinian Jews, Jews from Bokhara, Palestinian Arabs, and others. The project of political Zionism was not to recognize this pluralistic nature of Palestine. The claim over the land of Palestine was justified using a political slogan framed by Herzl "A land of no people for a people with no land."[23] Realizing the nature of plurality and diverse communities living communities in the land, Lucien Wolf, a Jewish opponent of Zionism, had proposed that the allies of war time should make a declaration supporting the settlement of Jews in Palestine as a "refuge from persecution." Similarly, Edward Grey, Foreign Secretary, was proposing that an autonomous Jewish settlement in Palestine could be made. They both worked towards bringing Jewish consensus across the Western world - a bottom- up[24]approach. But, the Zionist Conversation prevailed over other views on Jewish settlement. The fruit of the Zionist Conversation was the "Balfore Declaration" (1917).

The model of Zionist Conversation, inferred from above discussion, seems to be denying every form of conversation which is in solidarity with the oppressed. It labels such conversations either as philo-Semitic or anti-Semitic. It does not allow room for critical and diverse approaches to live as communities sharing land and culture. In Asian context at large, similar phenomenon of labelling and silencing Conversational voices is ever increasing. Correspondingly "internal colonisation"[25] and violence on "internal colonies" is a growing phenomenon. Violence against women, both boy and girl children, increasing flesh trade, violence on tribes, adivasis, dalits and environment; constraining democratic spaces, – all are different internal colonies facing violence. Alongside the increase of internal colonies, the State governments spend huge money on the import of arms and justify the same in the name of National Security. It is all deliberate diversion of national debate that connects every Asian nation with the Asian realties. The need of the hour is to overcome such a phenomenon.

## Conversion into Zionism

"... line between racist conspiracy theory and Christian Hebraism was a thine one." [26]

Political Zionism is presented as Christian Zionism by a stream of scholarship for the reason that political Zionism using Christian Scriptures to convert Christian faith communities in favour of political Zionism. So called secular word "Philosemitism"[27] or "Philo-Semitism"[28] is used to explain such a phenomenon. Theodore Herzl is said to be the first person to use the word "Zion," name of a hill, also related to ancient stories of the Bible, imbuing it with political meaning. By doing so, he invoked the "ancient sentiment[29] of the "Promised land." After Herzl, Political Zionists continue to use the Bible to gain international support as well as justification for political Zionism. Weizmann has taken it further using the words "Jewishness and Zionism" interchangeably,[30] which is not a justified usage. "Jewish" has to do with one's religious beliefs and cultural practices, whereas, Zionism has to do with the political project of forming a Jewish State in Palestine. Weizmann realized that colonial rulers of the West, British in particular, were not welcoming the Zionist project, therefore, felt they needed to be converted into Zionism, as "philo-Semitics." He started to address the British in religious terms by saying "...the Bible, Jerusalem's book, influenced the city over two millennia after it was written. Britain was a Biblical nation."[31] He created a particular image of Jewishness among the secular rulers of Great Britain using the Bible, biblical themes of promised land, return to the promised land and biblical Israel and comparing these to contemporary Jewish people. In this wasy Weizmann could induce into the secular mind a religious notion of people by rooting them in the ancient sentiments of the Bible. Such a concept can be called philo-Semitism or a friend of Jews and means one who views and listens the way Zionists want them to. Zionist Conversation and Conversion into Zionism needs to be distinguished based on the understanding of the word "philo-Semitism" as explained above. Having understood the need for interaction between Zionist Conversation and Conversion into Zionism Weizmann stated appreciatively that the "... line between racist conspiracy theory and Christian Hebraism was a thin one."

Continuation of philo-Semitism is further observed in giving a name to the intended Jewish State. Some suggested "Judea or Zion," and some others "Ivriya or Herzliya".[32] It was Ben-Gurion's suggestion to name the new Jewish State "Israel,"[33]signaling a shift from "land of

Palestine to land of Israel," which logically convinces Christians across the world to equate the Biblical Israel with the contemporary Israel.

An interesting observation on Conversion to Zionism has to do with abandoning Jewish – Christian dialogue based on the teachings, life and ministry of Jesus Christ and Torah. Such teachings and practices have to do with inviting Jewish communities to embrace the teaching of Jesus Christ for discipleship, something referred in literature as "views of early restorationists."[34] But, Rev. William Hechler, Chaplin of the English Embassy, is said to have moved away from the restorationist position and replaced it with a new idea of "fulfilling Biblical Prophecy" with Jews occupying Palestine and Jerusalem.[35] He further defined Christian vocation as the task of seeing to it that Jews across the world come and occupy the land of Palestine.[36]

David Lloyd George, who became British Prime Minister in 1916, had keenly observed the theological shift in Great Britain, as discussed above using the word philo-Semitism, and the concept of "Conversion into Zionism." He had seen that Weizmann was able to strengthen British imperialist project of expansion and control, at the same time effectively use of "ancient sentiment" drawn from the Bible to justify political Zionism.

The agony is that many contemporary Christians in India have been converting themselves to political Zionism in the name of fulfilling Biblical Prophecy. This view is highly critiqued as "sacrilege," man's project in deciding over second coming of God and day of judgement. Dynamics of Christian Scriptures made visible through Biblical theology is being abandoned and the Bible is used to judge either "philo-Semitism" or "anti-Semitism." The Bible is further used to justify *Aliyah* and "occupation." Historical significance of Ecclesia, prophetic engagement in society seems to have lost into Hechler's thesis.[37] Tours to Holy places in Jerusalem is reduced to tourism- objectifying people and places, losing the importance of pilgrimage. Touring Christian friends hardly talk to the Palestinian Christians or Arabs, who love to share hospitality with Indians; our touring Christian friends hardly take part in Sunday worship with the Palestinian Congregation or Jewish Christian Congregation. It seems like prophetic diakonia is not counted as an criterion in critiquing ministries of Church.

## Prophetic Diakonia : A Way Towards Borderless Ecclesia

> No one can hope to make any effective mark upon his time and bring the aid that is worth bringing to great principles and struggling causes if he is not strong in his love and his hatred. I hate injustice, tyranny, pompousness and humbug, and my hatred embraces all those who are guilty of them. I want to tell my critics that I regard my feelings of hatred as a real force. They are only the reflex of the love I bear for the causes I believe in.[38]

Prophetic diakonia should not be mistaken for fortune sayings or as fixing a date for the Messianic second coming. Prophetic diakonia places itself in service of communities beyond any boundaries; communities that are otherwise divides based on race, caste, religion, nationalism and gender. Moreover, it enables the community to transcend the boundaries with a deeper commitment for the least and to hate the sinful structures that forms boundaries. At this juncture a word on the limitations of the efficacy of prophetic diakonia within a religious tradition is in order.

According to Dr. B. R. Ambedkar religion can be one of the agencies for transformation through its moral, ethical teachings aiming at transformation of a community.[39] At the same time any call by a nation or a community is much powerful than a call for justice by religion.[40] Therefore, religion hardly prevails on justice between communities. The prophetic diakonia aimed at borderless ecclesia is a justice question within the community as well as between the communities and nations. Religion itself can stand aloof from the aspirations that go along with organizing of the poor, excluded and marginalized communities in opposition to a borderless prophetic tradition.

In response to political Zionism the Church in the land of Israel-Palestine evolved itself into a movement called "Kairos Palestine," collaborating with peace movements from secular world upholding the cause to be borderless in the proper biblical prophetic tradition. It even invites the communities in Asia as well as Africa, particularly Churches from these continents to be partners with them.[41] Justice and equality are not just questions confined to particular regions but for the nations across the world, including questions on ecological justice. Having outlined initiatives towards the borderless in a prophetic diakonia tradition in Asia, let us move a step further and look at prophetic initiatives in India beyond Christian tradition and engage with such initiatives.

Indian Church is critiqued for its lack of prophetic diakonia as it sometimes adheres to boundaries of caste and parochial nationalism. Dr. B. R. Ambedkar raised a pertinent question why conversion to Christianity is not progressive in spite of long years of missionary investments?[42] In other words, why has the Indian Church failed to get "appreciation" of Indian masses? He reasoned out three hindrances that had prevented this, which I call boundaries. First impediment is the bad moral values of the British settlers in India. Secondly, struggles between the Catholic and Neo-catholic missions for supremacy, and finally wrong approach of the missionaries in propagating Christianity.[43] All the three reasons mentioned by Ambedkar points at Missionary Christianity in India, whether from the West or East which has been preoccupied with itself without asking what the marginalized communities of India require of Christianity. The converts to Christianity are predominantly from Untouchable castes and marginalized communities, says Ambedkar.

"It is necessary to bear in mind that Indian Christians are drawn chiefly from the Untouchables and, to a much less extent, from low ranking Shudra castes. The Social Services of Missions must, therefore, be judged in the light of the needs of these classes. What are those needs?"[44]

In other contexts Ambedkar mentions that,

> Untouchables take the nomenclature "Christian" in order to give themselves an accepted picture… There is a general attempt to call themselves by some name other than the 'Untouchables'… All of them if away from their localities would call themselves Christians."[45]

It all points at marginalized, Untouchable communities viewing Christianity differently from that of the Christian missionaries and they appreciated Christianity to some extent.[46] They seems to have seen Christianity as socially relevant to them. But Christian missionaries seem to have missed identifying aspirations and needs of its members and Untouchable communities at large.

On the issue of Christian morals and practices, as raised by Ambedkar, Indian Christianity is critiqued for its dualistic approach preaching equality of all on the one hand and adhering to caste segregation on the other. An important critique comes from Arya Samaj Sanathan Dharmi leader Pandith Lekh Ram and Swami Dayananda on Christian white *Padiri* (European missionary preacher). They expose dualism in the leadership of the white *Padiri*, who distances himself from the Untouchables in the presence of caste Hindus yet, preaches equality and brotherhood.[47] Lakh Ram's critique is a call to the converts to abandon Christianity and return to join Arya Samaj. The driving point to be inferred is that Christianity in India, in spite of its very long history of life and ministry did not hate sinful structures of caste system and practices of untouchability and failed in its collective response to the Gospel of Jesus Christ.

Taking the argument further, contemporary Ambedkarites critique the Indian Church for not nurturing the revolutionary spirit of its members, who come from Untouchable background, and instead theologically nurture them to be passive towards exclusionary practices.[48] Dr. Ambedkar says,

> In the theological age, the poor lived by the hope that spiritual forces would ultimately make the meek inherit the earth. In the secular age, otherwise called modern times, the poor live by the hope that the forces of historical materialism will automatically rob the strong of their strength and make the weak take their place.[49]

The morality and ethics of Christianity cannot be reduced to the individual alone by saying that Christianity is all about personal relationship between believer and God and its purpose is to reach heaven.[50] Asian and African societies are community based and not individual based. Therefore, the aspirations of communities need to be met theologically as well as socio- economically and socio-culturally. Any reduction of society and community in India, Asia, Africa into mere individuals means a moving away from the prophetic path to embrace liberal views of individual freedom and individuals accruing wealth. Prophetic diakonia needs to take adequate steps to service communities realizing community needs. At the same time it must continue to address caste boundaries and patriarchal boundaries.

On the question of "Christian Supremacy" different questions are raised from time to time. Firstly, Christian missionary activity is, as mentioned elsewhere,[51] likened to the expansion of colonial powers in Asia. Linking Christianity with colonialism is a dangerous project as it negates Christian vocation of prophetic diakonia. Such an assumption forms the basis to accuse Christian community as being non- patriotic. Sometimes even the social development, healing and educational work of the Church in India is criticised as a strategy for proselytisation. M. K. Gandhi says, "...While you (Christian missionaries) give medical help, you expect the reward in the shape of your patients becoming Christians."[52] On Christian social work Dr. B. R. Ambedkar however raised a different question to that of Gandhi:

> The Indian Christians need two things. The first thing they want is the safeguarding of their civil liberties. The second thing they

> want is ways and means for their economic uplift. I cannot stop to discuss these needs in all their details. All I wish to point out is that this is a great desideratum in the social work the Christian Missions are doing in India. [53]

While M. K. Gandhi's critique on Christian social engagement is a presentation of Christianity as a proselytising religion without social commitment, the question raised by Dr. B. R. Ambedkar belongs to the prophetic diakonia premise based on equality and justice with a vision to go borderless. It is pertinent from this discussion to pick-up appropriate questions from both the critiques of Christianity in India in order to radicalise the prophetic diakonia of the Church in India and pave the way towards a borderless ecclesia. Another aspect of the above discussion that needs to be inferred is to understand the needs of Christians from the Untouchable and marginalized communities. There is great need for the educated Christian leadership with a renewed commitment for this cause. A prophetic diakonia requires not just a reasoning tradition but an educational tradition that appeals to one's consciousness.

On Christian approach in planting the seeds of the gospel Dr. B. R. Ambedkar critiqued the missionary approach in choosing caste Hindus over the Untouchable communities. According to Ambedkar,

> The services rendered by the Missions in the fields of education and medical relief are beyond the ken of the Indian Christians. They go mostly to benefit the high caste Hindus. The Indian Christians are either too poor or too devoid of ambition to undertake the pursuit of higher education. High schools, colleges and hostels maintained by the Missions are, therefore, so much misplaced and misapplied expenditure from the point of view of the uplift of Indian Christians. In the same way much of the medical aid provided by the Missions goes to the Caste Hindus. This is especially the case with regard to hospitals.[54]

Ambedkar's critical voice on Christian missionary work in India is with adequate knowledge of Christian missionary practice of ignoring the needs of the marginalized, and Untouchables and is very much based on empirical survey of the time.[55]

In a way complementing Dr. B. R. Ambedkar's argument, Walter Brueggemann's reflections on the prophetic focuses on Christian liturgy and Biblical theology. Brueggemann says that we are not prophets as many seem to claim for themselves but we responsibly adhere to the prophetic tradition.[56] Moreover, prophetic doesn't mean finger pointing at others. Instead prophetic is a tradition that names sin which destroys forces that affirm fullness of life. In short, prophetic diakonia always transcends self- seeking wealth and fame and it invites one to commit for social transformation. Therefore, let the preaching ministry of the Church reflect upon the prophetic traditions found in the Scriptures and bring an awareness among worshippers on prophetic diakonia and the need to grow into a borderless ecclesia.

## Conclusion

In order to be borderless, exclusionary, exploitative, colonising systems of violence are identified as what constitutes borders in this article as. An important border concern in Asia from Middle- East namely political Zionism is explored using two variables "Zionist Conversation" and "Conversion into Zionism." Based on the said study, this paper identified Political Zionist influences imposing a culture of labelling and silencing democratic conversations and changing debate on Asian realities into parochial nationalism or spiritual nationalism, and encouraging the import of arms. Further it outlined how Indian Christians are manipulated with the use of Bible, ancient sentiment, ancient names of people and places drawn from the Bible. As a result, there seems to be a conversion of Christian community into Zionism in subtle ways. Tourism to Holy places is also a means of promoting conversion into Zionism. In such a changing Christian Church scenario a possible way to renew the Church life and witness seems to be prophetic engagement with the society at large and transforming self (Church) into borderless ecclesia. For the said purpose Ambedkar tradition is discussed as a way for the Indian Church to move ahead in prophetic tradition along with other Biblical, missionary and ecumenical resources at its disposal.

## Endnotes

[1] Quoted by D. C. Gill in D. C. Gill, *How we are Changed by War: A Study of Letters and Diaries from Colonial Conflict to Operation Iraqi Freedom* (London: Routledge, 2010), 7.

[2] Mohamed Kamel Dorai, "State, Migration, and Borders' Fabric in the Middle East." <file:///G:/State,%20Migration,%20and%20Borders'%20Fabric.pdf> (20 May 2018).

[3] Simon Sebag Montefiore, *Jerusalem The Biography* (London: Weidenfeld & Nicolson, 2012), 450.

[4] Montefiore, *Jerusalem The Biography.* Referring to the context of anti-Semitism of the time, Political Zionism is said to be born from the spirit of the French Revolution demanding individual freedom.

[5] Montefiore, *Jerusalem The Biography,* 450.

[6] Montefiore, *Jerusalem The Biography,* 450- 51.

[7] Montefiore, *Jerusalem The Biography,* 452.

[8] Montefiore, *Jerusalem The Biography,* 453.

[9] Naim Stifan Ateek, Cedar Duaybis, Maurine Tobin, ed., *Challenging Christian Zionism: Theology, Politics and The Israel- Palestine Conflict"* (Jerusalem: Sabeel Ecumenical Liberation Theology Centre, 2005), 25.

[10] Moses Hess, a comrade of Karl Marx in 1862, had raised the said question in his writings *Rome and Jerusalem: the Last National Question.* See also *Jerusalem The Biography,* 450. British colonisers, who ruled India held similar views to that of Moses Hess.

[11] Montefiore, *Jerusalem The Biography,* 460.

[12] Montefiore, *Jerusalem The Biography,*460.

[13] Montefiore, *Jerusalem The Biography,*460.

[14] Montefiore, *Jerusalem The Biography,* 494.

[15] Montefiore, *Jerusalem The Biography,* 494.

[16] Montefiore, *Jerusalem The Biography,* 452. Herzel is said to have believed what kind of Zionism is needed, and such a belief determined Zionist Conversation.

[17] Montefiore, *Jerusalem The Biography,* 494f

[18] Montefiore, *Jerusalem The Biography,* 493.

[19] Montefiore, *Jerusalem The Biography,* 495. Lord Balfour is mentioned as Zionist. This does not mean he did not support positivism. Therefore, his confession of Zionism is political and had nothing to do with religion or any love for the Jewish religion and practices; See also *Dr. Babasaheb Ambedkar Writings and Speeches* (New Delhi: Dr. Ambedkar Foundation, 1989), Vol. 5, 411.

[20]"The Balfoure Declaration, 1917" <http://www.balfourproject.org/wp-content/uploads/2016/11/The-Balfour-Declaration.pdf> ( 10 May2018).

[21] Montefiore, *Jerusalem The Biography,* 458-5.

[22] Montefiore, *Jerusalem The Biography,* 451.

[23] Ateek, *Challenging Christian Zionism.* 27.

[24] "The Balfoure Declaration, 1917" <http://www.balfourproject.org/wp-content/uploads/2016/11/The-Balfour-Declaration.pdf> ( 10 May2018); A movement called "Women in Black" is a resistance movement by Jewish women in Jerusalem and elsewhere, wherein women openly resist Jewish occupation of Palestine and the colonising of the land. Zionist Conversation label such as "Self -hating Jews."

[25] "Internal colonies" denote communities within a nation that are kept under unseen boundary lines, excluded from the main stream of national life, inflicted with violence and exploitation by the dominant categories or groups

[26] Montefiore, *Jerusalem The Biography,* 495.

[27]Stephen G. Burnett, *Philosemitism and Christian Hebraism in Reformation Era* (1500-1620), <https://digitalcommons.unl.edu/cgi/viewcontent.cgi?article=1112&context=classicsfacpub> (25 May 2018).

[28] Montefiore, *Jerusalem The Biography,* 495.

[29] Montefiore, *Jerusalem The Biography,* 450.

[30] Montefiore, *Jerusalem The Biography,* 451.

[31] Montefiore, *Jerusalem The Biography,* 495.

[32] Montefiore, *Jerusalem The Biography,* 571.

[33] Montefiore, *Jerusalem The Biography,*571.

[34] Ateek, *Challenging Christian Zionism*, 29.

[35] Ateek, *Challenging Christian Zionism,* 29.

[36] Ateek, *Challenging Christian Zionism,* 29.

[37] Rev. William Hechler was the Chaplin of the English Embassy and the thesis is that Christianity has a vocation to "fulfilling Biblical Prophecy" by facilitating Jewish occupation of Palestine and Jerusalem.

[38] Vasant Moon, *Dr. Babasaheb Ambedkar Writings and Speeches* (New Delhi: Dr. Ambedkar Foundation, 1989), Vol. 5, Introductory page.

[39] Vasant Moon, *Dr. Babasaheb Ambedkar,* 398.

[40] Vasant Moon, *Dr. Babasaheb Ambedkar,* 398.

[41] For Prophetic peace, democratic initiatives from the Israel- Palestine see Mary Stella, "Jerusalem: Shenanigans vs Peace Initiatives," in *People's Reporter* A Forum of Current Affairs Vol 31, Issue 01, Jan' 10-25,2018, 6.

[42] Vasant Moon, *Dr. Babasaheb Ambedkar* 430-440.

[43] Vasant Moon, *Dr. Babasaheb Ambedkar* 430-440.

[44] Vasant Moon, *Dr. Babasaheb Ambedkar* 452.

[45] Vasant Moon, *Dr. Babasaheb Ambedkar,* 419.

[46] Praveen PS, Perumalla, "Will you Walk yet another mile?" in *Preaching in the 21st Century: Towards a New Homiletics* (ed. Victor, Vinod and Amritha Bosi Perumalla; Delhi: ISPCK, 2013), 112-133; See also Praveen PS, Perumalla. "Camouflaged Dalithood: Telangana Experience and the Churches' Mission to Strive to Sustain, Renew and Safeguard the Integrity of Creation." in *Mission At and From the Margins: Patterns, Protagonists and Perspectives* (ed Peniel Rajkumar, Joseph Prabhakar Dayam, I. P. Asheervadham; Oxford: Regnum Books International, 2014), 97- 109.

[47] Kenneth W. Jones. ed., *Religious Controversy in British India: Dialogues in South Asian Languages* (Albany: State University of New York Press, 1992), 72- 74.

[48] *Bharatiya Crystvulaku Ambedkar Hecharika* (in Telugu) (Hyderabad: Samanthara Publications, 2017).

[49] Vasant Moon, *Dr. Babasaheb Ambedkar,* 396.

[50] For a detailed debate on this question of personal relationship between believer and God see Vasant Moon, *Dr. Babasaheb Ambedkar,* 406ff.

[51] K. M. Panikkar, *Asia and Western Dominance: Survey of the Vasco Da Gama Epoch of Asian History 1498-1945* (Kuala Lumpur: The Other Press, 1993).

[52] Vasant Moon, *Dr. Babasaheb Ambedkar,* 446. Quoted herein by Dr. B. R. Ambedkar

[53] Vasant Moon, *Dr. Babasaheb Ambedkar,* 453.

[54] Vasant Moon, *Dr. Babasaheb Ambedkar,* 452.

[55]Vasant Moon, *Dr. Babasaheb Ambedkar,* 452. Mr. Winslow's survey report on the "attitude of the intelligentsia of India towards Christianity" is quoted by Ambedkar.

[56] Walter Brueggemann, *The Practice of Prophetic Imagination: Preaching an Emancipatory Word* (Minneapolis: Fortress Press, Second print 2001), …

## Bibliography

Ateek, Naim Stifan, Cedar Duaybis, Maurine Tobin, ed. *Challenging Christian Zionism: Theology, Politics and*

*The Israel- Palestine Conflict".* Jerusalem: Sabeel Ecumenical Liberation Theology Centre, 2005.

Burnett, Stephen G. *Philosemitism and Christian Hebraism in Reformation Era* (1500-1620). <https://digitalcommons.unl.edu/cgi/viewcontent.cgi?article=1112&context=classicsfacpub> (25 May 2018).

Dorai, Mohamed Kamel "State, Migration, and Borders' Fabric in the Middle East." <file:///G:/State,%20Migration,%20and%20Borders'%20Fabric.pdf> (20 May 2018).

Gill, D. C. *How we are Changed by War: A Study of Letters and Diaries from Colonial Conflict to Operation Iraqi Freedom.* London: Routledge, 2010.

Jones, Kenneth W. ed., *Religious Controversy in British India: Dialogues in South Asian Languages.* Albany: State University of New York Press, 1992.

Montefiore, Simon Sebag. *Jerusalem The Biography.* London: Weidenfeld & Nicolson, 2012.

Moon, Vasant *Dr. Babasaheb Ambedkar Writings and Speeches.* Vol. 5. New Delhi: Dr. Ambedkar Foundation, 1989.

Panikkar, K. M. *Asia and Western Dominance: Survey of the Vasco Da Gama Epoch of Asian History 1498-1945.* Kuala Lumpur: The Other Press, 1993.

Peniel Rajkumar, Joseph Prabhakar Dayam, I. P. Asheervadham., eds. *Mission At and From the Margins: Patterns, Protagonists and Perspectives.* Oxford: Regnum Books International, 2014.

Stella, Mary "Jerusalem: Shenanigans vs Peace Initiatives," in *People's Reporter* A Forum of Current Affairs Vol 31, Issue 01, Jan' 10-25,2018.

Victor, Vinod and Amritha Bosi Perumalla., eds. *Preaching in the 21st Century: Towards a New Homiletics.* Delhi: ISPCK, 2013.

Walter Brueggemann, *The Practice of Prophetic Imagination: Preaching an Emancipatory Word.* Minneapolis: Fortress Press, Second print 2001.

__________ <http://www.balfourproject.org/wp-content/uploads/2016/11/The-Balfour-Declaration.pdf> (10 May2018).

__________ *Bharatiya Crystvulaku Ambedkar Hecharika.* (in Telugu. Hyderabad: Samanthara Publications, 2017.

4

# Revisiting Christian Mission Responses and Challenges of Hindutva Movement in a Multicultural Society:
## Towards A Borderless Ecclesia

**S. Soban Kumar Daniel**

One of the most comprehensive definitions of the Church's mission is that given by John Stott: "Mission describes everything the Church is sent in to the world to do"[1] Though this statement may sound too general he further added two more related statements.: 'Mission is not a word for everything the church does"; "Mission does not cover everything God does in the world". The primary purpose of the Church is to be a community living to the praise of his glory, worshipping God, listening to his word, and in the love which springs from the Godhead ministering to one another and serving the world.[2] God has no borders in his activities in the world.

Mission was in past decades a term associated with Christian missions and their activities. However, now the word is applied to many missions and not specifically to Christian missions. In India at the current time Christian mission and missionaries face both direct and indirect persecutions as the current ruling alliance of parties have seen it fit to bring in anti-conversion laws in some states and this has curtailed the work of Christian missions in India. In this scenario it is important to revisit or rethink about the witnessing life of every Indian Church and Christian mission in general by examining their broader witness in the face of borderless persecutions.

## The term 'Hindutva'

The Hindutva movement in India is a religious and political movement. "The Bharathiya Janata party (BJP), the Rasthtriya Swayam Sevak Sangh (RSS), and the Vishwa Hindu Parishad (VHP), as well as the militantly anti-Muslim Shiv Sena, are movements collectively seeking to establish a Hindu state in India. The central ideology of this political movement is Hindutva literally translated as 'Hinduness' – which seeks to establish the political, cultural and religious supremacy of Hinduism, the Hindu nation"[3].

The word "Hindutva" stands for both a political ideology and religious identity produced by a confederation of Hindu revivalist movements in the latter part of the 20th century. Its foundations lie in the continuation of a stream of thought within Hinduism which upholds Brahmancal interest, reaction to foreign rules and their impact on Indian culture, concerted effort to present Hinduism as a credible religion in the midst of modern challenges and a revival which has affected all aspects of Hindu life. What is known as the "politicisation of religion and communalisation of politics" has had a great deal to with the development of Hindutva movement. It is seen as a threat to the secular fabric of Indian politics and to the rights of religious minorities including Christians.

Against this context this paper is an attempt to analyse the Hindutva movement and the responses of Christian missions to explore the possibility of developing proper attitudes towards Hindus in the context of India today.

There are different views about the Hindutva movement. The Hindutva leaders try very hard to interpret the ideology and programmes of the movement as providing a true secular basis, stable political system and promising prosperous India. On the other hand, there are critics within the Hindu fold, secular thinkers and leaders of religious minorities who demonise the Hindutva movement and see it as a great danger.

There are several definitions and interpretations, yet it is not clear as to what Hindutva is. The Anti-Hindutva group like Fernandez and Bhatkal criticise the Hindutva movement saying, "Hindutva became known as the ideology of the Brahmins, a party of the Brahmins." They further opine that Hindutva is a traditional ideology whose social agenda is to uphold and implement the canons prescribed by Manu.[4] "In other words Hindutva is an ideology to keep caste discrimination intact to the benefit of upper castes. The BSP (Bahujan Samajvadi Party), primarily a Dalit party explicitly describes BJP as a Manuvadi party. This is in plain language calling Hindutva as castesim."[5]

Today Hindutva is explained as cultural nationalism. It is interesting to note that in the sense of religion "Hinduism' is not an appropriate term to express the 'eternal way of life' (*Sanatanadharama*), as many Hindus point out, because the term is derived from the name of the river Indus." In their view Hindutva is formed on the basis of castesim. But Golwalker who became the RSS chief in1940 gave the following advice:

> The non-Hindu peoples in Hindustan must either adopt the Hindu culture and language, must learn to respect and hold in reverence Hindu religion... or may stay in this country, wholly subordinated to the Hindu nation, claiming nothing, deserving no privileges, far less any preferential treatment- not even citizens' rights.

In one of the election manifestos of BJP, it defines Hindutva thus: "Hindutva is a unifying principle which alone can preserve the unity and integrity of our nation. It is a collective endeavour to protect and reenergize the soul of India". Further the BJP says that "The BJP is committed to the concept of one nation, one people and one culture. Cultural Nationalism of India which is the core of Hindutva."

The purpose of this paper is to present a balanced picture of the nature and development of Hindutva movement and its challenges by analysing the challenges it poses to the multi-religious and multicultural Indian society particularly to Christian mission. Some of the Christian approaches to Hinduism have been to a great extent critical and this paper will investigate the fundamentalist forces within Christianity in India and suggest a dialogical way of relating to Hindus within the frame work of Christian mission. This is also an attempt to highlight the Christian response to the Hindu revivalism and to explore the possibilities of developing proper attitudes towards Hindus in the propagation of Christian mission in India today.

The Hindu revivalist movements and their challenges to the secular fabric of the nation and for the Christian minority need to be looked into more objectively. There are conflicting standards and counter arguments in the practice of Hindutva. Therefore, we need to analyse this critically, and evolve a dialogical approach. The problems of the Christian minority in the post-independent India are a recurring feeling of insecurity and a fear because of communal attacks and persecution. Through this paper various socio-cultural and religious issues will be identified that need to be addressed both by the Hindu majority and the Christian minority.

## Christian Mission Responses: An Investigation

There are certain Institutions that represent the church at national level. The Catholic Bishop's Conference of India (CBCI) represents the Catholic community which forms about 50% of the Christian population.

First we will present a proper view of mission history as it has been exaggerated by the Christians and twisted by the proponents of

Hindutva movement. We will try to achieve a balance with relevant factors.

Second it is important to recognize the damage caused by Christian fundamentalist groups in the name of mission with a mushrooming of new movements and sects and a missionary competition and confusion created on the ground. Many such groups are supported by fundamentalist groups from outside of the country. Then the question is what is the kind of mission the church is called to do without taking the fundamentalist line or liberalist line.

Thirdly we will point out the importance of Hindu Christian dialogue. Hindu –Christian dialogue has a long history with different dimensions. We have to point out both the prospects and the problems. We will look at good practices and present the hopes and aspirations of a few involved dialogues.

The Hindutva critique is that the Christian missionaries came to India to proclaim the gospel and mission in conspiracy with British imperialism during the colonial rule. But if this were so one only needs to look at the numbers to understand that despites several centuries of strenuous Christian mission with institutional power we have left only a tiny minority of Christians in India. This question must therefore be addressed concretely by the Christian community with the facts and numbers.[6] Colonial rule in India has not made a great impact on conversion to Christianity. If colonial rule and the contribution of Christian missionaries in the form of health and education have encouraged propagation of Christianity and conversion, it is surprising that the effect has not been greater than a Christian population of 2.4% as a whole. If this was the determining factor, the number of schools and colleges that were constructed by the colonial rulers and the missionaries should have added to the percentage of Christians in India to a great extent.

Regarding this, Arun Shourie says:

> On the surface there were many disagreements between British administrators and the Missionaries, and between them and the ideologists. There were disagreements within each group too: among ideologists for instance. A surface reading therefore suggests a tugging and pulling in different directions. But in fact none of these groups had any difference over the ultimate objectives – the conversion of the heathens to Christianity, and the extension and perpetuation of British rule.[7]

Shourie further adds:

> And so the effort to civilize India, to secure it for the British empire, to gather it up as the rich harvest for the Church proceeded as a joint endeavour: the civil servants helped by many devices, including among these their 'religious neutrality': 'the soldiers of the Cross' reinforced each other's efforts; and the scholars helped, working to 'undermine' and 'encircle' and thereby prepare the way for the 'soldiers of the Cross' to 'finally storm' 'the strong fortress of Brahmanism".[8]

Vishal Mangalwadi has responded to the charges made by Arun Shourie as follows:

> The East India Company was formed in the year 1600. By 1757 it had become the dominant political force in India. You must be familiar with the facts that- Thousands of Indians flocked to live in the British settlements such as Surat, Madras, Bombay and Calcutta; tens of thousands worked in the British factories and homes; they even served the Company's army against the Indian rajahs, and yet no Englishman thought that converting their Indian servants would strengthen their hold on India. During the entire seventeenth century only one Indian is known to have been baptized by the chaplains of the company ... During the entire eighteenth century, not a single British missionary was permitted to work in the British territories. The only protestant mission that existed in India was started by the Danes in the non-British territory in Tranquebar. A few of their German missionaries were later tolerated in some British centres because they had earned great respect from the Hindu and Muslim kingdoms around them... In 1793, when it was discovered that William Carey was travelling to India to serve as a missionary, he was disembarked from the British ship. He had to come on a Danish boat, and then work as a manager in an indigo plantation, partly in order to evade arrest. Finally, in order to work as a missionary, he

> had to settle in the Danish territory of Serampore. ...The unbridled religious liberty for missionaries of all religious shades was wrested from the British parliament only in 1833. It took 46 years to force England to allow Western missions to operate freely in India. ... In 1813, a law was passed that missions could operate in India, but only under license. At the same time, the East India Company was asked to spend Rs.100, 000 from its profits for public education in India. The British destroyed existing education, until 1835 this grant was used almost exclusively for promoting Sanskrit, Persian and Arabic. No grant was made available for mission work; at least 26,589 Hindu temples were receiving financial support from the company in the Bombay presidency alone...[9]

Therefore it is clear that the colonial rule did not encourage conversion to Christianity either through government rulers or through any inducements in the form of development works.

Even today the Christian mission needs to fulfill its prophetic role by increasing the Christian flow of justice by developing more and more educational institutions and mission hospitals to provide services to the needy and to the under privileged. Christians should focus on increasing commitment to liberation of weaker sections in society. This commitment to the downtrodden urgently calls for a constructive strategy in civil society.

Hindutva forces raise the question of missionaries' commitment to the poor. They say that their ultimate aim was for conversion and numerical expansion. Setting aside this charge, at the same time the Christian mission must admit that sometimes they failed to help the poor in most occasions due to their limitations on various fronts.

In recent tmes many Christian Institutions that were started to help the poor have betrayed this trust without serving the poor and weaker sections of the community. They serve the rich. For instance, Christian colleges, schools and hospitals meant for the poor and underprivileged 100 years ago, to a large extent serve the rich now.[10] Christians need to examine our commitment to the service of the poor.

Notwithstanding the arguments put forward by Vishal Mangalwadi, there were a number of instances in which mass conversion happened with the aid of the British missionaries and the colonial rulers. For example, in Travancore, many missionaries raised their voice for the elimination of slave-trade and the colonial rulers finally listened to them. As a consequence there was a mass conversion in Travancore.[11]

## Christian Fundamentalism and Mission

The Christian fundamentalist view that Christ is the only way of salvation is a dominant image of Christianity. According to Gnana Robinson, "Christian fundamentalism has been the pioneer for all the fundamentalist groups".[12] Although Churches have rendered many social activities, various Christian fringe groups have done aggressive proselytisation.[13] On many occasions Christian fundamentalist groups have abused other religious traditions in public and betrayed the image of Christianity. For the public, there is no distinction between the mainline Churches and the fringe fundamentalist groups, so they just assume this is the behaviour of all Christians. However we cannot ignore the fact that the mainline Churches too cannot be totally absolved of such aggressive evangelism. Mainline churches too organize evangelical meetings during which sometimes things are said that denigrate the religious values and traditions of other religions. The Pentecostal missions give primary importance to conversion rather than doing mission. This is certainly not helpful for a sincere and open dialogical relationship with larger secular society.

In countries like India, various Church denominations have developed the practice of organizing evangelistic preaching through conventions and meetings. This has become a common feature especially during summer holidays. This has mostly resulted in creating tension between Christians and other faiths. Independent preachers at these summer conventions use loudspeaker systems. This results in confrontational preaching by the local Hindus. Today, similar practices are being adopted by people of other faiths. This is because some present Christians are converts from Hinduism and they assume that similar conversion is still possible through preaching and evangelistic work. A strange combination of preaching the gospel and engaging themselves in mission was used by both fundamentalist and mainline groups for similar reasons. For example, can Christians justifiably sing that "Christ is Lord of all" without the permission of Hindus and Muslims?

There was a polarization between the evangelical side and the dialogical side in terms of the ideology of conversion and related matters. Some felt this approach confused people and needed clarification. For example, in the name of evangelism some attacked Hindus as worshippers of the evil spirits and Muslims as followers of rigid and ruthless rules. In the name of tolerance, Hindus repeated, untiringly, the slogan that all religions possess equally valid ways of salvation, and in the name of correction, Muslims highlighted the unforgivable sin of worshipping Jesus and calling him God.

Being "evangelical" means "bringing good news to others". But we need to reflect on how to share the good news of God's love being revealed in Jesus Christ in words and actions that are not arrogant and triumphalist. Does this not include an element of calling people to a new orientation in life, following Jesus and living in Christ? In Christian mission, evangelism and inter-faith dialogue are "two sides of the same coin". In the process of dialogue a Christian explains his faith. He will only use words to preach the gospel. Therefore, it is more an explanation of faith rather than a real dialogue. In such situations how can genuine dialogue be achieved? Jesus called all sorts of people to follow him. Can the church represent the collective charisma of the fellowship of equals? Why does this fundamental word "evangelical" provoke a frown? Fundamentalism or religious fanaticism in any form needs to be viewed as the enemy of the preaching of the gospel. Further, the Church needs to review its understanding of evangelism.

Evangelism is not the conversion of people from one religion to another; rather evangelism is the struggle against evil in the society, thereby changing the orientation of human beings with the values and the concerns of the kingdom of God.[14] To this end, there is a need for re-examination and reformulation of mission praxis.

However, some religious groups see the conversion of others to their religion as a matter of religious obligation or faith to their religion. Therefore, they attempt to win over others to their religion. For them, religious freedom is construed as permission to proselytise. It should be emphasized that this is a matter of religious conviction of a particular belief and theology. One community's freedom of religion is in fact another religious community's violation of freedom of religion.[15] Those who oppose proselytisation say missionaries with colonial power, used inducements such as health care, education and access to jobs to convert people. Thus they weaken or destroy the native culture and value system. This is a violation of cultural rights and religious freedom.[16] At the same time, the activity of proselytisation threatens religious freedom today. The balance between religious identity and the right to choose a religion is practically difficult to attain in a pluralistic society without harmony between religious communities.[17]

In India, it is easy to notice the mushrooming of sectarian churches with different labels and approaches that has created missionary competition and confusion. Essentially they are fundamentalists favouring selected verses from the Bible and interpreting them literally. Some Christians want to cleanse them and try to educate them in proper way of the scriptural teachings.[18] This kind of Christian fundamentalism is not only irritating to the thinking of normal Christians but also the people of other religions, particularly Hindus. In the name of Christian mission, many Churches are encouraging fundamentalist groups within them. They also betray Christianity by diluting theology and its universal vision and mission. If there is a misconception about the church and suspicion about its mission in the minds of Hindus and others, it has to be explained lucidly and evidently.

## Towards an Indigenous Christianity and Hindu Christian Dialogue

There is a need to have constructive intra-religious dialogue among Christian communities to correct their errors and mistakes. A clear understanding of religion is important for a multi-faith context such as India. Thereby Christians can be witnesses to the peace of God, empowered by the Holy Spirit and prove that 'all may be one' without any divisive spirit in the multi-religious society. In this situation, creative and constructive dialogue can play a vital role to sustain the principles of Christian mission and Dialogue.

An authentic dialogue between evangelicals and ecumenicals in the country seems to be impossible mainly because each group has powerful support from abroad. No conversation can be held because there is no common ground or a common expression to hold a serious and constructive dialogue.[19] A solution given here is dialogue or mutual education that means we learn from each other. This will be helpful to social change and nation building.

As far as India is concerned, the current misuse of religions, religious fanaticism and communalism call for the immediate attention of all as religions continues to be more effective at inspiring conflict than peace. It appears to be true that religions are used for political gains. In this situation, the future of Christianity in secular India lies in liberal Christians, co-operating with open- minded Hindus and at the same time denouncing hostility and fanaticism.[20]

Hindus and Christians should work together for the life of people who are struggling and suffering on an ongoing basis in their daily life.[21] But there is a need for inter-religious cooperation in pursuing common purposes like human rights and freedom.[22] There are some Christians who are actively committed to the struggle against injustice in the society who are seriously involved in movements of liberation together with people of other faiths, who believe that they participate in this work in the name of Christ.[23] Therefore, Christians' main work is to help people's ongoing search for their identity in their struggle for justice and freedom. In a multi-religious context this option will provide the necessary grounding and a direction that would integrate the concrete prophetic concern. This situation sustains an inter-religious response and cooperation.[24] Thus we need to envisage and hope for a new community, which is an inclusive community. This community will find sharing and partnership with mutual enrichment and growth. And there will be no domination or subordination, superiority or inferiority among the communities.[25]

The love of God can awaken a creative cooperative spirit. In this spirit we can face our common problems as a community together. The mutual acceptance will eradicate religious indifference.[26]

We need mutual correction for doing greater service to humanity with peace and non- violence.[27] The concern of inter-religious dialogue enables us to work together for upholding a secular ethos and secular forces against communalism. By this way, people of all faiths need to find practical efforts deeply committed to peace and socio- economic justice that are imperative concerns of the secular society.

The Christian community in Jesus Christ should be seen as a gift of God for humanity. Realizing this truth, Christians should not permit their faith to be abused for such distorted purposes in a multi- religious context. Christians are expected to build common humanity.[28] God did not leave himself without a witness. Hence in times of crisis, a faithful Christian has to become a friendly neighbour and helper to every human being irrespective of religion, caste and race.[29] Christians in India should actively get involved in affirming the reconstruction of modern India as a strong and vibrant nation. The Church must be a borderless church that collaborates with government agencies and other secular organizations to bring more life to the downtrodden people of India.[30] And religious and spiritual interaction can be done without abandoning one's own convictions.

Religiously plural countries like India simultaneously emphasize inter – faith relations as well as mission. But this brings a lot of confusion in the minds of the general public. What we need to realize is that clarification of issues within the Christian community alone is inadequate. Given the social and political consequences of the work of mission and conversion, the matter needs to be clarified in the public sphere. Otherwise Hindutva forces will strengthen further their political strategy of stigmatization.[31]

Effective witness of the Christian minority in secular India is emphasized. At the same time, we have also observed and identified some problems in maintaining these suggestions. But there are tensions in bringing these vision and mission in the Churches, which are already divided. Christian churches need to have a biblically balanced view of mission and, conversion and national identity. Adequate orientation at different levels would be required. Obviously the Church has failed to fulfill its mission in Christ's way although nobody can expect it to be perfect while it is placed in a complex and challenging situation.

## New Directions and Issues

Summing up the whole analysis of the problems of the Christian mission to construct a borderless Church, we may conclude that the problem of the Christian community is essentially people's problem. This is the problem of discrimination, inequality and injustice in the name of religion. The need of the hour is that all religious people need to come together as a joint effort irrespective of their own identities with mutual respect and recognition to support the Christian community and try to discover the possibility of equality and justice in socio-political, economic, cultural and religious life. If they are side-lined the problem will grow worse.

In this situation, as we have observed, for Christians political identity has become a question of character. The recent heavy attack and persecution of Christians by the Hindu extremists is flagrant in secular India. Powerful groups for economic gains focus on religious communities for persecution and exploitation in the name of religion.[32] Thus the problems of Muslims and Christians in India are more than the other religious minorities.

There is a missionary competition and confusion in the Indian scene compounded by a mushroom growth of fundamentalist groups, which complicate the scene further. Although all these socio- political factors contributed to the problem of conversion in India, this problem is connected with a conflict between two dissimilar and opposite religious systems.[33] At the same time The Mission and gospel work of some fundamentalist groups creates problems by their improper mission methods. The only aim to convert people from one religion to Christian religion must be avoided and this basic principle of fundamentalist group must be condemned. That will avoid tension between Christian and Hindus. Also the Christian Churches themselves are not free from distortion and corruption. Churches need to do rigorous self-examination through constant reflection and analysis of contemporary challenges to Church and society.

## Conclusion

To build up a borderless Ecclesia, the Christians should support and uphold the values of secular democracy. Otherwise the Hindutva group would pursue Hindu Rashtra, which would be disastrous for the religious minorities. At this situation, creative and constructive dialogue can play a vital role to sustain the principles of secularism. It can help to promote secular society through religious values and secular visions. For this, there is a need to mobilize all religious resources towards the making of our nation. Christians as individuals and groups should participate in order to fulfill their responsibility for the emancipation of the suffering people from social disabilities.

We need to critically examine their exclusivist claims and adopt a more positive and realistic attitude towards other religions in order to sustain. We need to review our understanding of salvation in the light of the Bible.

## Endnotes

[1] John R. W. Stott, *Christian Mission in the Modern World* (Downers Grove,IL: Inter Varsity Press,1975), 30.

[2] Krik. J. Andrew, *Contemporary Issues in Mission* (Birmingham: Clarkprint,1994), 2.

[3] Brenda Cossman and Ratna Kapur, eds., *Secularism's last sight?: Hindutva and the (Mis) Rule of India* (Delhi: Oxford University Press, 1999), 6-7.

[4] Gnana Robinson, *Challenges and Responses* (Bangalore: Asian Trading Corporation,2000) 141.

[5] Gnana Robinson, *Challenges and Responses.*141.

[6] L. Stanislaus "Gospel and Culture, Encounter in the Life of People" in *Indian Journal of Evangelization.* Vol. V, no.2 (April – June. 2000), 52.

[7] Arun Shourie, *Missionaries in India: Continuities, Changes, Dilemmas* (New Delhi: ASA Publications, 1994), 57 -58.

[8] Arun Shourie, *Missionaries in India,* 132.

[9] Vishal Mangalwadi, *Missionary Conspiracy* (Cumbria, UK:OM Publication,1998), 129- 130

[10] Nirmal Minz, *Rise up, My people and Claim the Promise: The Gospel among the Tribes of India* (Delhi :ISPCK, 1997), 85.

[11] K.K. Kusuman, *Slavery in Travancore* (Trivandrum: Kerala Historical Society, 1978), 11.

[12] Quoted in Samartha.J. Stanly, "Christian community in a Pluralistic Society: Towards a Revised Understanding", *Laity Focus and News (*20 Nov.1995), 3.

[13] Felix Wilfred, *Leave the Temple: Indian Paths to Human Liberation* (New York: Maryknoll, 1992), 186 - 187

[14] Roger Gaikwad, "Equipping the Church for its witness vis- a- vis Religious Pluralism and Fundamentalism and increasing Marginalization for the Poor", *Journal of Tribal Studies,* Vol V, no 2(July – Dec.2001), 45.

[15] Kusumita Pederson P. "Religious Freedom, the Right to Proselytize, and the 'Right to be Let Alone' " in *The World's Religions after September 11* Vol

2: *Religion and Human Rights* (ed. Arvind Sharma; Westport, CT: Praeger, 2009), 175-183.

[16] Kusumita Pederson P. "Religious Freedom",175-183.

[17] Kusumita Pederson P. "Religious Freedom", 175-183.

[18] Susan Bayly, "Christians and Competing Fundamentalisms in South Indian Society" in *Accounting for Fundamentalisms. The Dynamic Character of Movements (ed.* M. E. Marty and R. S. Appleby; Chicago: University of Chicago Press, 1994), 732.

[19] Stanley J. Samartha, "Christian Community in a Pluralist Society" in *Laity Focus and News (*20 Nov.1995), 4.

[20] Stanley J. Samartha, *Between Two Culture – Economical Ministry in a Pluralist World* (Bangalore: Asian Trading Corporation, 1997), 160.

[21] Stanley J. Samartha, *Courage for Dialogue, Ecumenical Issues and Inter-Religious Relationships* (Geneva: WCC, 1981), 156.

[22] Stanley J. Samartha, *Courage for Dialogue,* 30

[23] K. C. Abraham, *Third World Theology: Paradigm Shift and Emerging Concerns in Confronting Life: Theology out of the Context* (New Delhi: ISPCK, 1995), 206.

[24] K. C. Abraham, *Third World Theology*, 208.

[25] Parvey F. Constance, "Identity and Relationship in New Community", *The Community of Women and Men in the Church, A report of the World Council of Church* (Geneva: WCC, 1983) ,109.

[26] Nels F.S. Ferre, "Christianity among the Religions", *South Indian Church Man* (Sept. 1962) 9.

[27] Hans Ucko, "Introduction to the 'Thinking Together' Consultation on Religion and Violence", *Current Dialogue* 39 (June 2002), <http://wcc-coe.org/wcc/what/interreligious/cd39-01.html>

[28] Jutta, Sperber, *Christians and Muslims: The Dialogue Activities of the World Council of Churches and their Theological Foundation* (Walter de Gruyter: GmbH & Co, 2000), 277.

[29] Jutta, Sperber, *Christians and Muslim,* 273.

[30] L. Stainslaus, "Gospel and Culture, 47.

[31] Felix Wilfred, *Leave the Temple*, 189.

[32] Bhagwan Das, *Human Right and Constitutional Right* (New Delhi: the Asian Centre for Human Rights,1987), i-ii

[33] Sebastian Kim C.H, *In Search of Identity: Debates On Religious Conversion in India* (New Delhi: Oxford University Press, 2003), 188.

## Bibliography

Abraham, K. C. *Third World Theology: Paradigm Shift and Emerging Concerns in Confronting Life: Theology out of the Context.* New Delhi: ISPCK, 1995.

Andrew, Krik. J. *Contemporary Issues in Mission.* Bimingham:Clarkprint, 1994.

Bayly, Susan. "Christians and Competing Fundamentalisms in South Indian Society." Page 732 in *Accounting for Fundamentalisms. The Dynamic Character of Movements. Edited by* M. E. Marty and R. S. Appleby. Chicago: University of Chicago Press, 1994.

Constance, Parvey F. "Identity and Relationship in New Community." Page 109 in *The Community of Women and Men in the Church, A report of the World Council of Church.* Geneva: WCC, 1983)

Cossman, Brenda and Ratna Kapur., eds. *Secularism's Last Sight?: Hindutva and the (Mis) Rule of India.* Delhi: Oxford University Press, 1999.

Das, Bhagwan. *Human Right and Constitutional Right.* New Delhi: the Asian Centre for Human Rights,1987.

Ferre, Nels F.S. "Christianity among the Religions", *South Indian Church Man* (Sept. 1962) 9.

Gaikwad, Roger. "Equipping the Church for its witness vis- a- vis Religious Pluralism and Fundamentalism and increasing Marginalization for the Poor", *Journal of Tribal Studies,* Vol V, no 2(July – Dec.2001), 45.

Kim C.H, Sebastian. *In Search of Identity: Debates On Religious Conversion in India.* New Delhi: Oxford University Press, 2003.

Kusuman, K.K. *Slavery in Travancore.* Trivandrum: Kerala Historical Society, 1978.

Mangalwadi, Vishal. *Missionary Conspiracy.* Cumbria, UK:OM Publication,1998.

Minz, Nirmal. *Rise up, My people and Claim the Promise: The Gospel among the Tribes of India.* Delhi: ISPCK, 1997.

Pederson P, Kusumita. "Religious Freedom, the Right to Proselytize, and the 'Right to be Let Alone' " Pages 175-183 in *The World's Religions after September 11* Vol 2: *Religion and Human Rights.* Edited by Arvind Sharma. Westport, CT: Praeger, 2009.

Robinson, Gnana. *Challenges and Responses.* Bangalore: Asian Trading Corporation, 2000.

Samartha, Stanley J. *Between Two Culture - Economical Ministry in a Pluralist World.* Bangalore: Asian Trading Corporation, 1997.

Samartha, Stanley J. *Courage for Dialogue, Ecumenical Issues and Inter-Religious Relationships.* Geneva: WCC, 1981.

Samartha, Stanly J. "Christian community in a Pluralistic Society: Towards a Revised Understanding." *Laity Focus and News* (20 Nov.1995) 3-4.

Shourie, Arun. *Missionaries in India: Continuities, Changes, Dilemmas.* New Delhi: ASA Publications, 1994.

Sperber, Jutta. *Christians and Muslims: The Dialogue Activities of the World Council of Churches and their Theological Foundation.* Walter de Gruyter: GmbH & Co, 2000.

Stanislaus, L. "Gospel and Culture, Encounter in the Life of People." Page 52 in *Indian Journal of Evangelization.* Vol. V, no.2 (April – June) 2000.

Stott, John R.W. *Christian Mission in the Modern World.* Downers Grove, IL: Inter Varsity Press, 1975.

Ucko, Hans. "Introduction to the 'Thinking Together' Consultation on Religion and Violence." *Current Dialogue* 39 (June 2002) <http://wcc-coe.org/wcc/what/interreligious/cd39-01.html>

Wilfred, Felix. *Leave the Temple: Indian Paths to Human Liberation.* New York: Maryknoll, 1992.

# 5

# Borderless Ecumenical Attempt in Bible Translation

## Ecumenical Interconfessional Tamil Bible

**David Joseph Raj**

Throughout history, the Bible has always been in the hands of the powerful with regard to its interpretation and possession. During the pre-reformation period, the Bible was still a Latin version, and the Roman Catholic Church forbade Bible reaching ordinary people. Up until the year 1486, Berthhold, the Arch Bishop of Mentz debated on whether 'German language is capable of expressing what great authors have written in Greek and Latin on the high mysteries of the Christian faith? Certainly, it was not, hence they invented new words, or use old words in sacred Scriptures. This was how the Bible was always protected by the clerics and powerful in its version (language). One needs to bear in mind that there were diverse Christian texts that never made it into the canon.[1] The Council of Trent not only prohibited the translation of the Bible in vernacular languages but also took control of the interpretation stating that only the Church has the sole right to interpret the Bible. During the $14^{th}$ century, the dominant perception was that for the laity having direct access to the

Bible was not necessary to grow spirituality. In this paper, I would like to bring out the historical development of the Tamil Bible translation, an ecumenical attempt in common translation, and its impact on inter-Church cooperation[2] in India.

## The Pioneers of the Tamil Bible Translation

The first serious and systematic rendering of the Hebrew and Greek text of the Scriptures into Tamil was undertaken by Philipus Baldaeus at Jaffna in Sri Lanka.[3] He was a chaplain of the Dutch during the years 1656-1658. The Dutch army captured Sri Lanka. He left Sri Lanka in 1665 after living there for a very short period. During his stay he completed the translation of the Gospel of Mathew and the Creed was printed in 1671 at Rotterdam however, his translation of the gospel was never printed. After his translation work, another Tamil Bible translator in the seventeenth century was Adrianu de May, who belonged to the same Reformed Church as Baldaues. His translation work was recorded in the minutes of the Consistory of the Dutch Reformed Church of 29 May 1740 and it appears that he may have completed the translation of the entire New Testament into Tamil. But this translation was never printed. These two works existed in manuscript form and later Tamil Bible translators used this work.[4]

## Ziegenbalg and Schultze's Tamil Bible Translation

Bartholomew Ziegenbalg with his companion Henry Plutschu landed in India on July 1706. Ziegenbalg mastered the Tamil language and started the Tamil Bible translation work. Through his untiring work, Ziegenbalg completed the translation of the first Tamil New Testament on 21 March 1711 and it was published in 1715. In a letter to Halle, Ziegenbalg wrote that "All the books of the New Testament are now translated; this is a treasure in India which surpasses all other Indian treasure."[5] Ziegenbalg's Tamil Bible translation was in two parts. The first part included the four Gospels and the Acts of the Apostles. At that time paper was a very expensive commodity. Therefore it was decided by the missionaries at Tranquebar to use smaller print for the rest of the New Testament. There were four hundred copies printed of each part. The second part was brought out in 1722 with marginal references. He had started the translation of the Old Testament but unfortunately before he could not complete the work he died on 23 February 1719. At the time of his death, he had completed the Book of Ruth.[6] This rest of the translation was later completed by Benjamin Schultze on 24 November 1725 and it was published in Tranquebar in 1728. The first Tamil Bible was widely used among the congregations and there was a great demand for this translation.[7]

## Johann Philip Fabricius'[8] Tamil Bible Translation

Fabricius landed in Cuddalore on 28 August 1740 and started revising the Tamil New Testament Bible by Ziegenbalg in 1752. In spite of the prevailing political unrest, he spent all the powers of his mind on the task of Tamil Bible translation as well as a Tamil grammar and a most valuable Tamil dictionary. His translation of the Tamil New Testament Bible was published by SPCK Press, Madras in 1773, and the Tamil Old Testament Bible was published in 1777. J.S.M. Hooper said that:

> Fabricius crept through the original Bible text on his knees as if he were himself a poor sinner and mendicant, carefully weighing each word to see how it might best be rendered and the result was that, especially in the Old Testament, as later revisers and scholars have agreed, his rendering is again and again more faithful than either the English or the German. Little wonder that his work has been the basis of all subsequent revisions, and that the Lutherans have retained it in preference to the later versions almost to the present day; among them it is still known as the 'Golden Version'.[9]

## Serampore Printing Press[10] and Tamil Bible Translation

After Fabricius Tamil Bible translation work, William Carey and his friends Joshua Marshman and William Ward concentrated their interest in Bible translation work in all Indian languages. The British and Foreign Bible Society was formed in 1804 and they felt the need for Bible translation work in India. Therefore they encouraged missionaries to learn Indian languages and Bible translation works. Buchanan reported in his memorable journey in 1806 in the Tamil country that "there was a great cry for Bibles. The Tamil people followed him crying, we don't want bread or money from you, but we want the word of God."[11] The Tanjore missionary J.C. Kohlhoff expressed that "there were upwards of ten thousand Christians in Tanjore and Tinnevelly districts alone who had not among them one complete copy of the Bible, and that not one Christians perhaps in a hundred had a New Testament Tamil Bible."[12] In 1811, Henry Martin preached in Calcutta. In his sermon, he shared "this poverty of the word of God" and makes an appreciative reference to the Fabricius version.[13] Soon after there were five thousand Tamil New Testaments printed in Serampore.

## Charles Theophilus Rhenius' Tamil Bible Translation

The British Bible Society and Foreign Bible Society gave the first project of Tamil language Bible translation to Charles Theophilus Rhenius. He was born German in 1790 and died in 1838. He had come to work under the Church Missionary Society in Tinnevelly. In 1825, he brought out the New Testament in parts i.e the Gospels and the Acts of the Apostles. The entire New Testament was published in 1833. In 1840 the Bible Society published its first edition of the whole Bible in Tamil (the Old Testament consisting of the translation of Fabricius and the New Testament translation of Rhenius). Fabricius' Tamil Bible translation was far more accurate and close to the originals but his language was sometimes obscure. Rhenius' Tamil Bible translation, on the other hand, was chaste in idiom, though his renderings were often periphrastic and departed from the usual translations without sufficient warrant.[14]

## Peter Percival's Tamil Bible Translation

Peter Percival started his missionary work in Jaffna, Sri Lanka in 1826 and he brought out a Tamil Bible translation. In this translation work, he was assisted by the Tamil scholar and the father of Tamil modern prose Arumuga Navalar. A multi-national group of scholars Samuel Hutchings, H.R. Hoisington and Winslow (the most popular Tamil dictionary was named after him) was in the Tamil Bible translation team. The translation work was started in 1840 and this translation version was published in 1850.[15]

This version was not acceptable to the British Foreign Bible Society, Madras and the was rejected by the Bible Society for the following reasons:

1. The new version did not follow the original text.
2. The Tamil style in India was different from the Tamil of Jaffna, Sri Lanka.
3. The grammar used in Jaffna translation was different from the one prevalent in India and Tamil Nadu.
4. There were too many Sanskrit words in this translation.[16]

Thus the Peter Percival translation that was meant to be "Union Version" finally ended up as "Tentative Version".

## Henry Bower's[17] Tamil Bible Translation

In 1853 the British Foreign Bible Society recommended the formation of a new committee for the preparation of a translation acceptable to all Tamils in North and South Tamil Nadu as well as in Sri Lanka. In 1857, Henry Bower was appointed as the chief translator of this new committee. He commenced his Tamil Bible translation work in 1858. This project was assisted and associated by Muthiah, the brother of H.A. Krishnapillai, R. Caldwelll from Ireland, author of the famous '*A Comparative Grammar of Dravidian Philology*', Sargent from France and W. Tracy from the USA. The Tamil New Testament Bible was released in 1864 and in 1867. The entire Tamil Bible was published in 1871. The popularity of this version is known by the fact that this is the only translation that has been accepted by all non-Catholic denominations and this Henry Bower version is known as 'Power Version'.[18]

## The Tamil Bible Translation in the Twentieth Century

In the 20th century, the pace of translation of the Bible into Tamil quickened. There were a lot of attempts and enormous translation work done by various committees. Nor is there any indication that this translation has yet come to end. Bible translation into Tamil language in the present century began with the publication, in 1904 of the translation work done by Roman Catholic Bishop Bottero, Bishop of Kumbakonam, assisted by others. This translation was based on the Vulgate and included deuterocanonical books. In 1917 the when the second edition was published it was known as "Trinical's Version" and remained the most popular in Roman Catholic Churches up to 1970. After 1970, Professor Legrand of St. Peter's Seminary, Bangalore assisted by others, translated the New Testament and published it. This translation was based on the Greek New Testament, not the Latin Vulgate and the Old Testament with deuterocanonical books followed.[19] On the Protestant side, the Bible Society of India and individuals formed committees and launched a new Tamil Bible translation projects in 1923.

The following versions are remarkable:

## L.P. Larsen[20] Version

L.P. Larsen (1862-1940) known as "missionary of missionaries" translated the Bible with the help of G.S. Duraiswamy Pillai (1883-1965) originally based in Palayamkotai, Tirunelveli, and both moved to Madras in 1924. They began to publish trail editions of the Tamil Bible New Testament. For the first time, the Lutherans and others co-operated in the work of revision. While Fabricius' version of the Tamil Bible used the word *Paraparan* for God, later versions of the Tamil Bible used *Devan* for God. The Larsen version committee agreed to use the word *Kaduvul* for God. They published Tamil Bible

New Testament in 1928 and the Old Testament in 1936. There was a lot of criticism and protests, therefore, another version that would satisfy the original purpose of the Larsen Version, without evoking unnecessary criticism, seemed called for.[21]

## C.H. Monahan Version

C.H. Monahan (1869/71-1963) was assisted by H.K. Moulton and Bishop Stephen Neil. He undertook the revision of the translation of Larsen's version. The New Testament was issued in 1954 and the full Bible published in 1956. The new version met with a better response than Larsen's version, partly because a new generation wanted to read with a new vision. The words *Karthar* and *Kadavul* replaced *Yehowah* and *Devan* respectively used for God by Bower version.[22]

## D. Rajarigam Version

In 1947 there was a strong movement to remove Sanskrit influences from the Tamil language. It was argued that being one of the oldest Indian languages, Tamil could stand without Sanskrit. In addition to this, the language of the Union and Revised versions were considered "missionary Tamil" or "Christian Tamil" and therefore not fully satisfactory. D. Rajarigam and his colleagues, A.E. Inbanathan, Dhyanadan Francis, V.P.K. Sundram and A.R. McLaushen undertook a new translation project. This project was sponsored by the Bible Society of India. The New Testament was published in 1975. This translation was known as the New Translation or the Common Language Translation. In spite of the beautiful style and accuracy of this translation, it was not accepted by the majority of Tamil speaking Christians.[23]

## The Catholic Version[24] of the Tamil Bible Translation

The Catholic Version of Tamil Bible New Testament in the form of Arulappa Version translation work started in 1956 and it was released on 1 March 1970. The Old Testament translation work was completed in 1972. In November 1965, the Second Vatican Council issued the "Dogmatic Constitution on Divine Revelation" with its statement:

> easy access to Sacred Scripture should be provided for all the Christian faithful … and if, given the opportunity and the approval of Church authority, (if) translations are produced in cooperation with the separated brethren as well, all Christians will be able to use them.

In June 1968 the post-Vatican II spirit of fellowship and mutual acceptance, the Vatican Secretariat for Promoting Christian Unity and the United Bible Societies came out with the document "The Guiding Principles for Inter Confessional Cooperation in Translating the Bible". This becomes the *Magna Carta* (Great Charter) for all Ecumenical Biblical Translations including *Tiruviviliam* (first Inter Confessional Tamil Bible) published in 1995.

## The Ecumenical Inter Confessional Tamil Bible Translation

The Bible Society of India (BSI) and the Tamil Nadu Bishop's Council (TNBC) jointly organized a consultation on 23 November 1972 at the CSI Synod meeting hall, Chennai. It was decided to follow the "Guidelines for Inter Confessional Co-operation in Translating the Bible". There was a follow-up consultation on 20 June 1973 at the Jubilee Annexe of the Bible House, Bangalore. The programme for a common Tamil Old Testament was worked out. In 1974, Fr. R.J Raja (TNBC) and Rev. D. Rajarigam (BSI) were appointed as Convenors of this translation panel. The committee processed three books in 1976 (Ruth, Jonah and Proverbs). On 27 September 1976, A.E. Inbanathan and Fr. Michael Irudayam had the privilege of presenting these trial editions to Pope VI at Rome. In 1978 Fr. Michael Irudayam and Rev D. Jones Muthunayagam were appointed co-ordinators of the project. In 1980, the project was extended to the whole Bible and renamed as "Inter Confessional Tamil Bible Project". The entire translation work was completed in May 1993. The full Bible (Old Testament (OT), New Testament (NT) & Duetro Canonical books) was published in

1995 by the TNBC and the United Bible was released under the title *Tiruviviliam* or Common Translation/Inter Confessional Tamil Bible. In 2000 January the Plenary Assembly of CBCI granted permission for translation and publication of the Tamil Ecumenical Bible. [25] At present the *Tiruviviliam* Tamil Bible is used by various denominations, for example, the CSI Kanyakumari Diocese is adopting *Tiruviviliam* in their Worship and the Sunday School syllabus and the Tamil Nadu Theological Seminary, Madurai is using the *Tiruviviliam* in their theological studies. The Tamil speaking Christian peoples belonging to all the denominations are now using *Tiruviviliam* in their worship, personal devotions and daily readings. This is a good sign of ecumenical cooperation among the Churches.

## Conclusion

Regarding the historical journey of the Tamil Bible translation, I. Henry Victor raised an important question: Why the multiplicity of translations? He gave four answers:

1. The growth and constantly changing nature of the language into which the Bible is translated;
2. The discovery of older and more reliable biblical manuscripts which make earlier translations inaccurate;
3. The increased scholarly knowledge of the Hebrew and Greek Bible;
4. The development of new principles of translation [26]

Languages constantly grow and change. The Tamil language is no exception. Henry Bower, the chief translator of the Union Version realized this fact when he began his translation in 1873. At that time he noted that "the use of the Sanskrit letters in the writing and pronouncing of Sanskrit works" was increasing in official papers and books written by Indians.[27] The linguistic and social reformer Periyar, a Tamil scholar, introduced pure Tamil (i.e. without Sanskrit words) in schools, colleges, magazines, and books. The changes that take place in Tamil usage in India are reflected in changes in Sri Lanka as well. Therefore in order "to preserve the meaning of the original message, the form of language should be altered from time to time so as to adjust the content of the message to the constantly changing form of expression".[28]

Henry Bower's Union Version is the oldest translation in common use and the most popular among the Protestant Tamil Christians. The formal translation principle was used in making this translation. Its language is not the contemporary Tamil language. Moreover, it contains numerous Sanskrit words that are not used today among Tamils. The NT of the Union version is based on the *Texus Receptus*. After Bower's version, the Revised Version formed, it is the equivalent of the English Revised Standard Version. This version too follows the formal translation principle. Its language is similar to that of the Union Version, except that grammatical errors found in the earlier version had been removed. The Roman Catholic Translation is the version in current use that contains the Apocrypha (referred to as the deutero-canonical books by Roman Catholics). The language of this translation is beautiful, attractive and contemporary. However, the form of the proper names is unfamiliar to the Protestant Christians. Although the dynamic equivalence principle was used in making this translation, it was not consistently applied.[29]

Here I conclude with I. Henry Victor quotation:

> The historical journey of the Tamil Bible Translation indicates both that the need for new translations is felt more or less continually. It also indicates that the new translations, whatever their technical and artistic merit, are not always well received by the Christian people themselves. More study is needed to understand why this is so.[30]

Bible translation work reflects the socio-historic situations at the time of the translation. Ziegenbalg and Schultze were the pioneers in this venture, in 1871 Bower Version, in 1949 Revised Version, and in 1973

Roman Catholic Version were remarkable milestones of the Tamil Bible translation work in India. In 1995, the first Tamil Ecumenical Bible *Tiruviviliam* Inter Confessional Bible was published. This will pave the way for more cooperation between the Churches. This Ecumenical Bible translation venture will inspire other writers and scholars, not only to get nearer to the word of God but also make the Words of God"That they all may be one John 17:21," come true.

## Endnotes

[1] *The Bible in Many Tongues* (London: The Reliogious Tract Society, 1853), Cited in R.S. Sugirtha Rajah, *The Bible and the Third World: Pre-Colonial, Colonial and Post-Colonial Encounters* (Cambridge: Cambridge University Press, 2001), 46-47.

[2] The Roman Catholic Diocese of Sivagangai Bishop S. Edward Francis explains the term inter-Church cooperation: "the Christian missionaries from all over Europe and United States have come one after another in India to enhance the presence and beauty of the Word of God in Tamil Nadu. The Roman Catholic Church made a pioneering attempt in the apostolate of the press, it joined late in the Tamil Bible translation but in the end of the 20th century the Roman Catholic joined with other protestant Churches to form a committee to publish inter-Church/inter-confessional Tamil Bible.

[3] Tamil people in Sri Lanka and India first encountered the Gospel through the ministry of the Roman Catholic missionaries during the early part of the sixteenth century. However, they did not make any effort to translate and print the Bible into Tamil until the nineteenth century. Therefore the protestant missionaries were pioneers in this field. I. Henry Victor, "A Brief History of the Tamil Bible," *Indian Church History Review* (Vol. XVIII, 1984), 106.

[4] I. Henry Victor, "A Brief History of the Tamil Bible," *Indian Church History Review* (Vol. XVIII, 1984), 107.

[5] I. Henry Victor, "A Brief History of the Tamil Bible," *Indian Church History Review* (Vol. XVIII, 1984), 107-108.

[6] The first Tamil version of the Old Testament was printed in 1723 and contained the Books of Genesis to Judges. The Psalms were printed separately in 1724, and the Books from Ruth to Song of Solomon excluding the Psalms were printed in 1726. In 1727, the Books from Isaiah to Malachi were printed.

[7] J.S.M. Hooper, *Bible Translation in India, Pakistan and Ceylon* (Bombay: Oxford University Press, 1963), 71.

[8] Johann Philip Fabricius was born in Germany, Jura in 1710 and he studied in Halle. He died on January 23, 1791.Sabapathy Kulandran, *History of the Tamil Bible,* (Tamil) (Bangalore: Bible Society of India, 1967), 89,102.

[9] J.S.M. Hooper, *Bible Translation in India, Pakistan and Ceylon* (Bombay: Oxford University Press, 1963), 73-74.

[10] William Carey, missionary of the Baptist Missionary Society reached Bengal in November 1793, and after five years of uphill work in managing an indigo factory, in preaching, teaching, language study and translation, he along with his friends Joshua Marshman and William Ward, in 1800 eembarked upon their great task of translating and printing the Bible Scriptures in many languages in India. They edited and issued following language Bible translation works: 1805 Chinese, 1811 Malayalam, 1813 Tamil, 1814-1835 Malay, 1815 Burmese, 1815-1820 Batta, 1823 Sinhalese, 1829 Javanese, 1839 Urdu, 1841 Persian. J.S.M. Hooper, *Bible Translation in India, Pakistan and Ceylon* (Bombay: Oxford University Press, 1963), 15-26.

[11] J.S.M. Hooper, *Bible Translation in India, Pakistan and Ceylon,* 75.

[12] J.S.M. Hooper, *Bible Translation in India, Pakistan and Ceylon,* 75.

[13] J.S.M. Hooper, *Bible Translation in India, Pakistan and Ceylon,* 75.

[14] J.S.M. Hooper, *Bible Translation in India, Pakistan and Ceylon,*75-76. & S. Michael Irudhyam & Y. Robinson Levi, *History of Tamil Bible Translation* (Madurai: Theological Education through Living Literature, 2002), 41.

[15] J.S.M. Hooper, *Bible Translation in India, Pakistan and Ceylon,* 76.

[16] S. Michael Irudhyam & Y. Robinson Levi, *History of Tamil Bible Translation* (Madurai: Theological Education through Living Literature, 2002), 42.

[17] Henry Bower was born in 1812 in an Anglo-Indian family in Madras. He was a missionary of the Society of the Propagation of the Gospel (SPG). He translated into Tamil Tom Butler's anthology, Pearson's Creed, a Biblical and Theological Dictionary, Lectures on the Moral Law, the History of Christianity in India, and other works. He died in 1885 at Palayamkottai, Tirunelveli.

[18] S. Michael Irudhyam & Y. Robinson Levi, *History of Tamil Bible Translation,* 42.

[19] I. Henry Victor, "A Brief History of the Tamil Bible," *Indian Church History Review* (Vol. XVIII, 1984), 112. Apart from the work of the Bible Society there have been individuals who have translated the Bible on their own. One such person was N. Gnanapragasam, whose translation of the New Testament was published in 1922. S.T. Jebagnanam, made a translation of the Gospel of Mark in 1964.

[20] L.P. Larsen, was the first principal of the United Theological College (UTC), Bangalore. Bishop Azariah wrote that, "it is more accurate, more

concise in style, and more idiomatic than all the versions in general use - a Bible nearer to the original than any of its predecessors." I. Henry Victor, "A Brief History of the Tamil Bible," *Indian Church History Review* (Vol. XVIII, 1984), 113.

[21] J.S.M. Hooper, *Bible Translation in India, Pakistan and Ceylon,* 77-78.

[22] S. Michael Irudhyam & Y. Robinson Levi, *History of Tamil Bible Translation,* 54.

[23] I. Henry Victor, "A Brief History of the Tamil Bible," *Indian Church History Review* (Vol. XVIII, 1984), 113-114.

[24] The Tridentine Ecumenical Council during the first phase (1545-1547) affirmed that "the revelation of Jesus Christ could be passed along in both Written Scriptures and Unwritten Traditions". The Bishops also declined to approve vernacular translation of the Bible. This Council also confirmed that the Canon consisted of: Old Testament including Deutro-Canonicals (46 books) and New Testament (27 books). And the *Latin Vulgate* was to be the only approved text for doctrine, preaching and worshiping. *Providentissimus Deus An Encyclical letter from Pope Leo XIII:* In the nineteenth century, many questioned the divine origin and truthfulness of the Bible. In this Encyclical, pope Leo XII solemnly affirmed that the entire Bible is God's Word, holy and true. Pope also outlined a strict scientific method for studying the Holy Books. This Encyclical bore great fruits in the following years. S. Michael Irudhyam & Y. Robinson Levi, *History of Tamil Bible Translation* (Madurai: Theological Education through Living Literature, 2002), 55.

[25] S. Michael Irudhyam & Y. Robinson Levi, *History of Tamil Bible Translation,* 59-60.

[26] I. Henry Victor, "A Brief History of the Tamil Bible," *Indian Church History Review* (Vol. XVIII, 1984), 114.

[27] The change in Tamil has been particularly rapid since Indian Independence. Since 1947, as mentioned earlier, the Tamil-speaking people have tried to wean themselves from the influence of Sanskrit. The Sanskrit words such as *Visuwasam* faith, *Isuwariyam* wealth, *Vasthiram* cloth - these words replaced in the common translation work that uses *Nambikai* faith, *Selvam* wealth, *Aadaic* cloth for the same words in contemporary Tamil.

[28] I. Henry Victor, "A Brief History of the Tamil Bible," *Indian Church History Review* (Vol. XVIII, 1984), 115

[29] I. Henry Victor, "A Brief History of the Tamil Bible," *Indian Church History Review* (Vol. XVIII, 1984), 117-118.

[30] I. Henry Victor, "A Brief History of the Tamil Bible," *Indian Church History Review* (Vol. XVIII, 1984), 117-118.

## Bibliography

Hooper, J.S.M. *Bible Translation in India, Pakistan and Ceylon*. Bombay: Oxford University Press, 1963.

Irudhyam, S. Michael & Y. Robinson Levi. *History of Tamil Bible Translation*. Madurai: Theological Education through Living Literature, 2002.

Kulandran, Sabapathy. *History of the Tamil Bible*, (Tamil). Bangalore: Bible Society of India, 1967.

Sugirtharajah, R.S. *The Bible and the Third World: Pre-Colonial, Colonial and Post-Colonial Encounters*. Cambridge: Cambridge University Press, 2001.

Victor, Henry I. "A Brief History of the Tamil Bible." Pages 106-118 in *Indian Church History Review* (Vol. XVIII, 1984).

6

# Rethinking Ecclesia: Christian Missions and the Borderless Church

**D. Isaac Devadoss**

Setting the context is important for any consultation. The concept paper from the General Secretary titled "Towards a borderless Church..." talks about the different usage of the word *Ecclesia* from Genesis to Revelation. The topic for this consultation is "Rethinking Ecclesia". Several questions come to mind. What is the need for rethinking Ecclesia now? Is there an urgent call or necessity for the Church to rethink its, structure and function? If this exercise is only a program to celebrate 500 years of Reformation then we cannot expect any change in our Church. But if there is a genuine search for a change in the present Church then we must be serious about our business and ask ourselves the pertinent questions: What do we want to change? What is the purpose of the change? Where do we start?

History always teaches good lessons. In this paper, I have briefly highlighted the historical development of Ecclesia in different periods and how those changes brought the change in the understanding of mission and Church. This learning may help us to understand the "Churchless Christianity" today.

## Jesus' Understanding of Ecclesia

In Matthew 16: 18, when he says, "I will build my Church, and the powers of death shall not prevail against it, Jesus is talking about the quality of the Church i.e. ecclesia being "the assembly of the faithful ones" which resembled the synagogue (organizational or structured assembly).

## Apostolic Period

Ecclesia is a Greek word defined as "a called-out assembly or congregation." Ecclesia is commonly translated as "Church" in the NT. In Acts 11: 26 ecclesia refers to those who were the members of the Church and Acts 2: 47 mentions "Those who were being saved". A similar understanding of synagogue where people gathered for worship was also in use.

## Constantine Period; The Nicene Creed

One of the earliest ecclesiological statements embraced by the Church is found in the Nicene Creed (A.D. 325): "I believe in one, holy, catholic, apostolic Church." Two of these words are of particular significance to this discussion: "catholic" and "apostolic." The recognition of the catholicity or universality and the apostolic succession of the Church was being affirmed. The Church became an organization and powerful body under Constantine.

## Medieval Roman Catholic Ecclesiology

Popes in the Middle Ages, especially Innocent III at the Fourth Lateran Council in 1215 and Boniface VIII in 1302, identified salvation with being sacramentally connected to Christ through the church and declared that "Outside the church, there is no salvation". Similar statements can be found in the Eastern Orthodox tradition. This doctrine was based on Jesus' words "Unless you eat the flesh of the Son of Man and drink his blood, you have no life in you" (John 6:53).

## The Reformation

One of the biggest theological challenges in the Reformation was to answer the accusation that the movement seemed to be an assault on the catholicity of the Church. Until then it was believed that the apostolic authority of the Church was conveyed and continued through the episcopal laying on of hands from Peter.

According to Luther, the true Church is apostolic, not because of an episcopal chain of the laying on of hands, but only when it teaches what the apostles taught. Protestant ecclesiology thus found its apostolic legitimacy through the doctrine of *Sola Scriptura*. If the apostolic message is proclaimed, then the Church is apostolic, and it shares in the mystical oneness and catholicity that are the marks of the true Church. For Luther, the true, organic Church has both a visible and invisible nature.

## Later Formulation

As the number of Reformation Churches grew, a new crisis of ecclesiology developed. Each new branch of Protestantism was forced to articulate its own understanding of the true marks of the church. The Augsburg Confession, for example, states that "the Church is the assembly of saints in which the gospel is taught purely and the sacraments are administered rightly". Similar declarations are made by the Church of England. The emerging Reformation Churches tended to affirm the spiritual nature of the Church, but they also set forth certain "marks" of the Church, which could be visibly embodied only in communities.

## Development of Indian Christian Theology of Mission in the Context of Nationalism and Indigenization

Some of the voices that arose in the Indian context both before and after Independence from the British Raj tried to articulate Christ and the Christian faith in terms that were relevant to the contextual socio-cultural and religious beliefs and practices in India. Some of those articulations are briefly highlighted below:

## *Robert de Nobili (1577 -1656)*

De Nobili who started his mission at Madurai from 1606 used an "accommodation" mission method which allowed new converts to keep their caste markers and other traditional practices. Raimond Panikkar in his 1964 book *Unknown Christ of Hinduism* articulated about Christ being very much present in Hinduism as found in the Vedas.

## *Kaj Baago*

Baggo raised some radical questions in 1966: Must Buddhists, Hindus and Muslims become Christians in order to belong to Christ? Do they have to be incorporated into church organizations that are utterly alien to their religious traditions? Do they have to call themselves Christians—a word which, to them signifies, a follower of the Western religion? Should they necessarily adopt the Christian traditions, customs, and rites which often have their root in Western culture more than in the gospel? Are all these things conditions for belonging to Christ? He answered all of these questions with a resounding "No!" He argued that,

> The Christian religion, to a large extent a product of the West, cannot and shall not become the religion of all nations and races. The missionary task of today cannot, therefore, be to draw men out of their religions into another religion, but rather to leave Christianity (the organized religion) and go inside other religions, accepting those religions as one's own, in so far as they do not conflict with Christ, and regarding them as the presupposition, the background and the framework of the Christian gospel in Asia. Such a mission will not lead to the progress of Christianity or the organized Church, but it might lead to the creation of Hindu Christianity or Buddhist Christianity.[1]

## *The Debate Between M. M. Thomas and Lesslie Newbigin*

In 1971, M. M. Thomas[2] published a landmark book entitled *Salvation and Humanisation.* It is an examination of issues related to the theology of mission seen from within the particularities of the Indian context. Central to Thomas's vision is a radical rethinking of ecclesiology. Thomas is concerned with the implications of a Church that becomes increasingly isolated from society. He, therefore, encourages the idea of a "Christ-centered secular fellowship outside the Church." He goes on to argue that a vigorous ecclesiology should embrace a view of the Church that can "take form in all religious communities" because it "transcends all religious communities."[3] The Church can "take form as a Christ-centered fellowship of faith and ethics in the Hindu religious community."[4]

Thomas insisted that there is a distinctive new humanity that belongs to Jesus Christ, but that this new humanity cannot be equated with the visible Church. Thomas was concerned with believers inside the visible community of Hinduism.

In contrast, Lesslie Newbigin[5] raises important questions about Thomas's ecclesiology. In *The Finality of Christ,* Newbigin insists that the Church must involve a "visible community." However, Newbigin wants to be clear that by "visible community" he is not merely embracing the notion that salvation in Christ is linked to mere "church extension" or the "exaggeration of the community." Instead, Newbigin argues that "a visible fellowship is central to God's plan of salvation in Christ, but God's plan of salvation is not limited to the visible fellowship." According to Newbigin, the proper balance is achieved when we realize that,

> true conversion involves both a new creation from above, which is not merely an act of extension of the existing community, and also a relationship with the existing community of believers."

Thus, while acknowledging that salvation comes from God and is from above, central to God's plan of salvation is the uniting of his redeemed people to a visible community.[6]

## *Other Voices*

According to Ralph Winter[7], Churchless Christianity is not only missiologically sound but also strategically superior to traditional churches. Winter says,

> Apparently, our real challenge is no longer to extend the boundaries of Christianity but to acknowledge that Biblical, Christian faith has already extensively flowed beyond Christianity as a cultural movement, just as it has historically flowed beyond Judaism and Roman Catholicism. Our task may well be to allow and encourage the people of other faith to follow Christ without identifying themselves with a foreign religion.[8]

## Conclusion

From a historical perspective, the existence of unbaptized believers in Christ who are not under the authority of the Church is not accepted as normative ecclesiology. The traditional Catholic view that outside the church there is no salvation certainly would not accept the notion of followers of Jesus who are not in any sacramental relationship with the Church. The Reformation and the subsequent creedal formulations that speak to ecclesiology reveal that, despite a vigorous rethinking of the doctrine of the Church, the Reformed Churches could not possibly comprehend or accept a person released from the doctrine and discipline of the visible Church. Indeed, virtually all Reformed Churches have insisted on at least the sacrament of baptism and the Lord's Supper as necessary signs of the visible Church. Most also insist on some organized authority of pastors, priests, bishops, or elders who preside over a defined gathered community. Thus, if Churchless Christianity is to be accepted, it clearly represents a departure from the historic doctrine of ecclesiology as espoused by Roman Catholic, Eastern Orthodox, and Reformed Churches.[9]

## Endnotes

[1] Kaj Baago, "The Post-Colonial Crisis in Missions" *International Review of Missions,* 1966.

[2] M. M. Thomas (1916–96), a well-known Indian theologian and ecumenical leader who, for many years, was the director of the Christian Institute for the Study of Religion and Society, in Bangalore.

[3] M. M. Thomas, *Salvation and Humanisation* (Madras: CLS, 1971), 13, 38, 40.

[4] M. M. Thomas, *Salvation and Humanisation* (Madras: CLS, 1971), 13, 38, 40.

[5] Lesslie Newbigin (1909–98), British missionary to India, ecumenical leader, and bishop of the Church of South India.

[6] Timothy C. Tennent "The Challenge of Churchless Christianity: An Evangelical Assessment" *International Bulletin of Missionary Research,* Vol. 29, No. 4: 173.

[7] Missiologist, the founder and director of the U.S. Center for World Mission, in Pasadena, California.

[8] Ralph Winter, "Eleven Frontiers of Perspective," *International Journal of Frontier Missions* 20, no. 4 (2003): 136

[9] Timothy C. Tennent "The Challenge of Churchless Christianity: An Evangelical Assessment" *International Bulletin of Missionary Research,* Vol. 29, No. 4:172.

## Bibliography

Baago, Kaj. "The Post-Colonial Crisis in Missions." *International Review of Missions.* 1966.

Tennent, Timothy C. "The Challenge of Churchless Christianity: An Evangelical Assessment." *International Bulletin of Missionary Research,* Vol. 29, No. 4: 173.

Thomas, M. M. *Salvation and Humanisation.* Madras: CLS, 1971.

Winter, Ralph. "Eleven Frontiers of Perspective." *International Journal of Frontier Missions* 20, no. 4 (2003): 136.

7

# Rethinking Ecclesia: Being Ministers of Prophetic Diakonia

**V.J. John**

"For even the Son of Man did *not come to be served, but to serve*, and to give his life as a ransom for many." (Mark 10:45, NIV)

"Rethinking Ecclesia" has been the focus of our attention for a while now in the CSI to perceive the Church anew in a culturally diverse and pluriform society in India at the dawn of the twenty-first century. This calls for a fresh understanding of the 'ecclesia' which is basic to a renewed perspective on the task of ministry. The current Indian setting with increasing polarization of the people on the basis of ideological differences, politics based on religious belonging and aggressive push for caste-based identity together seem to strike at the very root of freedom and liberty enshrined in the Indian Constitution. It is in this context that we need to ask, "What is a viable and relevant ministry of the church in such a context?" We shall briefly focus our attention on three aspects: firstly, the basis of ministry, looking at the biblical and theological understanding of ministry; secondly, an analysis of the practice of ministry as they are carried out in the present time and finally, some suggestions for a prophetic diakonia as a way forward towards building Christ-centered communities of fellowship and nurture without barriers in a society driven by polarities and divisions.

## Basis of Ministry: A Biblical and Theological Perspective

Jesus came proclaiming the message of the in-breaking of the reign of God.[1] He declared, "The kingdom of God is at hand" and invited people to repent and believe the good news (Mark 1:15). It is for ushering in the rule of God that Jesus lived and died. The challenge to his ministry was never to be side-tracked from this basic goal. His preaching as witnessed in the parables, his teachings on the Sermon on the Mount, his miracles of healing and exorcism, his passion, suffering, and death on the cross, and finally his resurrection and new life were all signs of the presence of the reign of God embodied in his life and ministry. Jesus did not come to begin a new religious faith. Rather he was a reforming religious preacher in the first century Palestine context within an apocalyptic environment.[2] The 'ecclesia' was already in existence (Acts 7:38) even prior to the arrival of Jesus. However, his preaching and healing and solidarity with the suffering masses brought about transformation and change within the Jewish community of the time. Jesus calls this new community as "ecclesia" as Matthew would testify. For Jesus said, "… I will build my church, and the gates of Hades will not prevail against it". (Matt 16: 18; cf. 18:15, 17-18, 21). However, later this community was forced to be separated from the Jews (John 9:18). They were called the "new" Israel (Rom 11:7, 26). The Gospels thus portray Jesus as the foundation and the builder of the church.

The ministry of Jesus as portrayed in the Gospels was to serve the needy, heal the sick, feed the hungry, drive out demons, and to offer community and fellowship to the excluded. The leaders of the Jews and the Romans sought positions of power and authority community and service within society and on their behalf: "You know that those who are regarded as rulers of the Gentiles lord it over them, and their high officials exercise authority over them." (Mark 10:42). But

Jesus sought to serve the needy: "For even the Son of Man did not come to be served, but to serve, and to give his life as a ransom for many." (Mark 10:45). Serving others was the motto of Jesus' ministry. He was never tired of doing good for others, even foregoing his own meals and rest (Mark 3:20 cf. 1:32-34). It is in the service of others that he laid down his life on the cross. Although he was pronounced innocent by Pontius Pilate (John 19:4-7), he was handed over to be crucified because of the Jewish antagonism towards his influence on people for the good that he has done for them.

The disciples, on the other hand, seem to have failed to grasp the importance of service. They sought positions of power and prestige as we do very often today. There were disputes among them with regard to who was greatest among them. They (James and John) said, "Let one of us sit at your right hand and the other at your left in your glory." (Mark 10:17) despite Jesus having already said at least three times in no uncertain terms that "the Son of Man has to suffer and to die in the hands of the elders, chief priests and teachers of the law and rise again on the third day". Disciples not only failed to comprehend Jesus' saying, but Peter even insisted that he should not suffer (Mark 8:31-33). On another occasion, Peter asked Jesus, "We have left everything to follow you, what will we get?" (Mark 10:28; Matt 19:27; Luke 18:28). The disciples became followers of Jesus but had always in mind that they would gain something. We need to ask ourselves, "What is the motif for our being in ministry?" Are we in it so that we can give ourselves to the service of the needy or is it just a means of making an easy living?

Ministry of Jesus involved solidarity with the rejected and neglected people, whether it was the prostitutes (Matt 9:10-11; John 7:53:8:11), tax collectors (Luke 15:1-2; 19:1-10), Samaritan woman (John 4: 1-42), leprosy-affected (Luke 17:11-19) or demon-possessed (Matt 8:28-34). He identified with their causes and concerns. He healed them, made them whole and restored them to their rightful place in society. It is in search of the freedom and liberation of these vulnerable and rejected ones that Jesus gave up his life. His life was lived in the service of those whom he served. He remained true to the words, "If a grain of wheat that falls on the ground does not die, it remains itself; but it dies it brings forth manifold fruit" (John 12:24). Is such an example not against much of our own efforts that seek to preserve and promote ourselves through our ministerial task?

Jesus confronted the powers who went against God's purposes for human life. He stood up against the rulers and authorities when they did not fulfill the role assigned to them. He even called Herod Antipas, the ruler of Galilee 'fox' (Lk. 13:32). The Pharisees and chief priests were always attacking Jesus because he questioned the source of their authority and the depth of their commitment to the cause of the ordinary masses (Mark 11:27-12:17). Jesus said to the Jews who boasted of their Abrahamic descent, "You are determined to kill me, a man who has told you the truth...." (John 8:40)

He stood for justice and fair play in all human relationships. Human bonds were not to be exploited for personal benefits and vain glory. Each human being was precious in the sight of God and each is to be respected and honoured as they are, whether women, children or elders, the sick, the poor or the disabled. Peace and reconciliation was the motif for all his actions. He said, "Peace I leave with you; my peace I give to you. I do not give to you as the world gives. Do not let your hearts be troubled and do not be afraid." (John 14:27). Again he said, "Therefore if you are offering your gift at the altar and there remember that your brother has something against you, leave your gift in front of the altar. First, go and be reconciled to your brother; then come and offer your gift." (Matt 5: 23-24). Worship and liturgy which is the dominant part of our ministry today are devoid of meaning if we do not simultaneously work for justice, peace and reconciliation.

Jesus listened to the cry of the needy, whether she was a Canaanite woman (Matt 15:21-28), a Samaritan (John 4:1-42) or a Roman gentile (Matt 8:5-13), whether a publican or a tax collector; whether demon-possessed or leprosy-affected. Cry of the poor was the pulse of his ministerial engagement whether working on a Sabbath day or breaking the perceived morals of the social and religious set up. He was open to helping people overcome struggles against forces of evil in order that they may attain life to the full measure. He said, "I have come that they may have life and have it to the full" (John 10:10).

The ministry of Jesus was a challenge to the establishment. He made friends with those whom the powerful rejected, he identified with the causes of the ordinary human person, spoke against injustice, overturned the legal and justice systems of the day. He worked for peace, harmony, and reconciliation in the midst of diversity and differences. His ministry was distinct from those of his contemporaries. He laid emphasis on life and witness as against rituals and traditions. He was not afraid of being different in the pursuit of his ministerial roles. He never sought to fit into the established roles of the religious systems. Rather, he continually questioned prevalent roles and practices. He critically appropriated traditions to suit his proclamation of the reign of God which had dawned in his ministry. He was critical of practices inimical to the causes and concerns of neglected and deprived masses. His life and witness challenged the prevailing practices of spirituality divorced from the realities of life.

## Ministerial Practice of the Church: A Brief Analysis

With the conversion of Paul and his missionary travels, house churches were formed in many of the major cities of the Roman world. Church was the place of a shared life (*koinonia*), a life in partnership (Phil 1:5). The community gathered for worship, prayer and fellowship as did the early Jerusalem church, where fellowship was shared and those with little means of support were helped (Acts 4:32-35). The Lord's Table was the best example of sharing as the Corinthian community was reminded in the Pauline admonition (1 Cor 11:17-22). As part of the body of Christ, the believing community also shared in the pain and suffering of its members. The Corinthian church and the Macedonian church collected offerings for the support of the brothers and sisters affected by famine in Jerusalem (2 Cor 9:1-5). They shared in the suffering of the apostles as well as helped in their need (2 Co. 1:7). Paul was supported by the church at Philippi while he was in imprisonment (Phil 4:13-18). It is in the context of the church and the faith community that the believers were nurtured and cared for, fellowship shared, faith encouraged, worship offered and basic human needs were met.[3] This gives a glimpse into the ministry of the early Pauline communities.

However, with the growth of the church also came problems in churches as evident in different congregations, such as Thessalonica, Galatia, Corinth and Philippi. Over time, due to expansion and political patronage, this informal gathering of believers for prayer, fellowship, and worship as house churches gradually developed into a very formal, rigid and hierarchical organization. A synthesis of Greco-Roman culture and the conversion of Gentiles made such adaptation easier. The organized structure of the church, on the one hand, helped the spread of the gospel around the Roman world through missionary engagements; while on the other hand, Christian faith began to lose its charm and depth in its bastion from where it spread to other locations. It is interesting to note that the community is no longer identified as "Christians", the name with which they were first called at Antioch (Acts 11:26) in the NT, rather, it is called the "church". This gathered group in the words of Waetjen, were to "manifest all the qualities of nomadic existence, faith, solidarity, strength and endurance… "[4]

The ministry of the church through its history has evolved from the Pauline understanding of a three-fold ministry of bishop, presbyter and deacon as appears clearly in the deutero-Pauline tradition (1 Tim 3:1-3). In the initial stages the division was more of a functional one: bishop served as the ruling elder, presbyter or pastor as the teaching elder and deacons were devoted to the ministry of service (Acts

6:1-7). As time progressed the distinctions between these various roles and functions become more pronounced and the role of the bishop became superior and that of the deacon of less importance in the hierarchical order with the pastor/presbyter in the middle. Ministry, however, is not confined to clerical ministry and function of the office. It is a diversified ministry in which every member of the congregation shares. It is only by a collaborative effort of the diverse gifts possessed by each of her members that a universal and mutual ministry motivated by love could be carried out.

However, from a separate set of ministries assigned to each, there began to emerge a craving to moving from one function to another until one reached the top of the hierarchical order. Elections in many a church today has become a very fiercely fought affair, all in the name of serving the people. It is our shame that, at least at times, those selected to occupy elevated positions of power neither qualify for the task nor have the vision and commitment to work for the cause of the masses. Much time is needlessly wasted on matters that are secondary to the call and purpose of ministry. Priority in ministry has shifted from serving Christ and shepherding the flock to one of working for the interest and promotion of the minister. There is hardly any time left for the needs of the ordinary congregation member.

Training of ministers has not helped matters either. Attempts at all-round development of a minister have increased the burden of both teachers and students. Yet the end product many a time is not as suitable for the pastoral role of the predominantly rural Indian churches. Students go through the motions of training without actually being affected by what is taught and learned. Teachers in theology who do not see it as a vocation and consider it more as a profession, have been less than a model for the youngsters under ministerial formation to be enthused by their lifestyle and devotion. It is often heard said, "There was too much emphasis on academics and very little emphasis on personal and spiritual formation" of a minister.

Areas of ministerial engagement have widened over the years. From being confined to liturgical and sacramental celebrations, the ministry has widened to include various other aspects such as working for the underprivileged, human rights, women's concerns, justice issues, inter-faith issues, gender and ecological concerns. This has had both positive and negative impact on the task of ministry. Ever increasing number of ministerial roles requires more time and energy on the part of the ministers. Meetings and conferences consume much of their time and energy. Care and concern for people do not figure any longer in the priorities of ministry. The positive effect is the broadening of ministerial concerns. More and more people thus come under the purview of the ministerial responsibilities of the pastor. The incorporation of women into pastoral roles was a very positive development in the area of ministry. Increasing their number would be an affirmation of the Church's commitment to providing better pastoral care of the congregation. The pastoral role has widened to incorporate even those who do not publically claim allegiance to Christ with the understanding of society as the parish of the minister.

With the widening scope of ministerial roles also came power and prestige associated with pastoral roles. There are people who are motivated to enter ministry not as a vocation to serve the needy but for the position and status it might offer in society. Church as an institution offers many avenues for enhancing power and position for those who seek it. Church Institutions and properties in many instances have become a bane than a blessing. Self-denial and serving the needy has taken a back seat. Church as a pilgrim community on the way no longer enthuses many of her ministers.

## Ministry as Prophetic Diakonia: Some Suggestions for Building Christ Communities

Jesus having called his disciples and trained them, sent them out for the task of mission (Luke 9:1-6; Matt 10:1-24; John 20:21). The task entrusted to the disciples were no different from what Jesus himself was doing. The Nazareth Manifesto sets out in detail the mission task of Jesus. "The Spirit of the Lord is on me because he has anointed me to preach good news to the poor. He has sent me to proclaim freedom for the prisoners and recovery of sight for the blind, to release the oppressed, to proclaim the year of the Lord's favour." (Luke 4:18-19) It was to this very same ministry that the disciples were sent out. Preaching the gospel and engaging in actions of social emancipation and the ecological mission all emanate from the mission task of Jesus. They were told to proclaim the good news and heal the sick wherever they would go and were received. He said, "As you go, preach this message: "The kingdom of heaven is near". Heal the sick, raise the dead, cleanse those who have leprosy, drive out demons. Freely you have received, freely give." (Matt 10:7, 8) Proclaiming the good news of the arrival of the kingdom in the person and work of Jesus and effecting the changes that the arrival of the kingdom mandates in the experiences of the sick and demon-possessed was the task of their mission engagement.

A prophetic diakonia should contribute towards helping to establish a transformed and transforming community centered on principles and values of Christ. The command of the risen Lord to his disciples and through them to all Christians is that the task to which they are called to engage is to make disciples of all nations (Matt 28:18-19) and to be a living witness to the risen Christ wherever they might live and work. It involved calling people without distinctions and differences to living a Christ-like life. Everyone was to be encouraged without discrimination to live as Jesus lived. The disciples were to bear witness to Christ through their life and work. Others were to take note of the distinctive lifestyle and value systems of disciples of Jesus as distinct from the religious practices of the Jewish leaders and the power games of the Roman rulers. Their task was not just converting as many people as were possible, but to influence people with the message of love and self-sacrifice that Jesus made in fulfilling God's purposes for his life. Following Jesus' example, the disciples were to be like salt and light, penetrating the evil and darkness around them through their life and action.

When Jesus said, "As the Father has sent me, I am sending you" (John 20:21), the mission and ministry of the disciples had to be no different from that of Jesus. A prophetic ministry calls for taking risks, walking unchartered paths. One of the problems faced in the church is that it is too traditional and always resistant to change. While traditions are important they should not be a hindrance towards progress and renewal.

During the course of her two millennia of existence the church has witnessed the mission that her Lord had entrusted to her through preaching (evangelism), teaching (educational institutions) and philanthropic work (hospitals, destitute homes, care centres, etc). While these have benefitted many lives and some have turned to Christ, at least some have failed in fulfilling their role. Renewed efforts are called for to make these arms of the church to serve the needs of ordinary human persons thereby promoting justice and equality.

Church's ministry should help establish inclusive communities, both within the church and in the wider society. Differences on the basis of confessions and diversity in ethnicity and language should help enrich the community than divide it. It should shed the image of being secluded communities (e.g. mission compound Christianity), cut away from other peoples and communities. The church cannot exclude people on the basis of ethnicity, language, sexual preference, gender, and caste. All people are called to be God's children. All deserve togetherness and belonging.

The church should become part of society that she lives in and engage with their problems and issues, providing a perspective of Christ to deal with them. The church should engage in building communities of peace and reconciliation where there is no disharmony or disputes.

Conflict resolution between peoples and communities should figure in the agenda of church's ministry.

Issues of justice and human rights should figure prominently in the task of ministry. Preaching and practicing justice within the church and her institutions and promoting the cause of justice within the wider society should gain importance in the ministerial roles. The church should be a community of justice and fair play. Without the practice of justice within her own spheres of influence, she cannot be a channel of justice, peace and reconciliation in the wider community. The church should effectively articulate her collective voice against unjust practices in society and the government.

Church today is too obsessed with power politics. Litigations, struggles for power and position, and property disputes have become the bane of church life in many of our congregations today. There is undue competition for power. Church elections are marred by corruption and nepotism. Long sermons on justice are often heard preached but hardly practiced even within its own spheres of influence. Church has drifted away from her call to be salt and light in a world of darkness and evil. It's a collective failure of the church that needs introspection and re-fixing.

Church is called to be a community of love and care, a community of inclusiveness, and a community of prophetic witness and ministry. The church cannot just confine its acts of love and care towards her own members but must expand it to the entire human community without distinctions of caste and class. Love and care are to be shared with all who might need it (Good Samaritan), especially the poor and vulnerable. Ministers and ministry should be concerned with the plight of the migrants, the excluded communities and the creation under distress. It is the act of love towards one another and care for the earth, our common home, that will make her known as Christian disciples to the rest of the world.

Church hence is a universal and ecumenical community driven by the same faith and the example of our Lord Jesus, despite differences of language, doctrines and culture. The church should be seen as the foretaste of an eschatological community than a mere sociological entity, although it is in the present social sphere the relevance of the ministry of the church is assessed. Fear and insecurity are the causes behind erecting barriers and building walls between peoples and communities. It is openness, transparency and shared love that makes walls and borders irrelevant to create a community of trust and mutual care. Let us commit ourselves to a prophetic ministry without fear or favour to make it one that is rooted in love and for the good and wellbeing of the other.

## Conclusion

The ministry of Jesus was to work to establish the rule of God in a community dominated and oppressed by the powers of Rome. He continued to struggle against the powers in bringing about transformation and change to the vulnerable people through his words and deeds. The "ecclesia" that was commissioned to carry on this task was faithful to her task in its early stages. Over the years the "ecclesia" through her external and outward growth became an institution where the voices of protest against injustice and violation of human rights have become muted. Serving vulnerable communities has become a mere slogan. The church needs to rejuvenate herself in following her Lord if she is to be effective in carrying out the ministry in a more complex world. The Indian situation is perhaps one of the most complex in the current circumstances. Let us, as the church and her ministers, with the aid of the Holy Spirit, commit ourselves to work for the cause of the vulnerable as the call of our ministerial engagement. To do so we cannot but be ministers of a prophetic diakonia.

## Endnotes

[1] J.D. Crossan, *The Historical Jesus* (Minnesota: Fortress Press, 1996), 256.

[2] "Christianity" in *Anchor Bible Dictionary*, Chief ed., David Noel Freedman, vol. 1 (Doubleday, 1992), 927.

[3] Ralph P. Martin, *The Family and the Fellowship: New Testament Images of the Church* (Exeter: The Paternoster Press, 1979), 34-45.

[4] Herman C. Waetjen, *The Origin and Destiny of Humanness: An Interpretation of the Gospel According to Matthew* (San Rafael, CA: Crystal Press, 1976), 173.

## Bibliography

Crossan, J.D. *The Historical Jesus*. Minnesota: Fortress Press, 1996.

Martin, Ralph P. *The Family and the Fellowship: New Testament Images of the Church*. Exeter: The Paternoster Press, 1979.

Waetjen, Herman C. *The Origin and Destiny of Humanness: An Interpretation of the Gospel According to Matthew*. San Rafael, CA: Crystal Press, 1976.

8

# Green Church Movements for a Sustainable Economy

**Mathew Koshy Punnackadu**

God's purpose in Christ is to heal and bring to wholeness not only persons but the entire created order. "For God was pleased to have all his fullness dwell in him, and through him to reconcile to himself all things, whether things on earth or things in heaven, by making peace through his blood shed on the cross" (Col.1: 19-20). The Church should work for a godly, just and sustainable economy which enables men, women and children to flourish along with all diversity of creation. We should be open to all models. We may accept one model as the starting point but we should be open to learning from the others as well, thus broadening and deepening our commitment to the renewal of God's creation.

Monastic Model Ascetic or monastic model is the oldest form of the Church's responses aimed at integrating some concerns relating to ecology as well as the crisis created by the misuse of the natural environment. Living in harmony with nature and keeping their needs to a minimum, the monastic communities proclaimed the message that the earth is the Lord's and that it should not be indiscriminately used to satisfy human avarice and greed. It was also a powerful protest against a wasteful lifestyle that was devoid of any responsibility to the world of nature. The Indian philosophical tradition culminates in an organic, holistic and spiritual world view and renunciative way of life. Hence, reduced consumption is an obvious outcome of such a philosophy. There emerges, thus, a pattern which is eco-friendly and sustainable.

Liberative Model Ecological liberation approach is based on the kingdom of God as preached by Jesus. Bringing about the kingdom of God is an active process of removing the sources of oppression and working towards the day when God's justice will reign in the human and non-human world. The Church must recognize and challenge the sinful socioeconomic and political systems that oppress the earth, its environmental systems and its people. The church in solidarity with the weakest, with that part of the creation that is victimised, seeks the renewal of the whole of creation. The Church has to declare its solidarity with groups like Chipko, Appico, Narmada Bachao Andolan (NBA), National Fishworkers' Forum (NFF), Karnataka Rajya Raitha Sangh (KRRS) and such that are struggling for ecological justice.

Eco-friendly Outlook- Study from Nature The resources in nature are finite or limited. These finite resources are used for an infinite period of time by getting constantly renewed. This is possible only if the resources are recycled. That is the reason behind cyclicity. One of the most inevitable results of this cyclicity is that all living and nonliving things get connected to one another. Such connected or interrelated things are involved in a constant process of "give and take". Every living organism accepts something either from another organism or from the environment, and in return gives something to it. eg. honeybee accepts honey from nature as her food, and helps in pollination). Environment maintains diversity. It doesn't allow one particular species to become dominant that it will affect the existence of other species. There is no VIP-ism in nature. Environment is a system which is "of all, by all, for all". Everything in nature is decentralized. Through decentralization, nature tries to divide the burden equally at all places. Food is produced or is available everywhere; water quenches thirst everywhere; waste is decomposed everywhere. Everything in nature is biodegradable. Human attitude is responsible for all the problems of environment. We only take everything from nature, there is no giving. Whatever goes away from us to nature is hazardous, toxic or non-biodegradable. This affects the natural cycles.

Catalyst in Building Up a New Economy The Church should act as a catalyst in building up a new sustainable economy. Building a new economy involves phasing out the old industries, restructuring the existing ones, and creating new ones. It is being replaced by efficiency gains in some countries; by natural gas in others, such as the United Kingdom and China; and by wind power in others such as Denmark. The new economy will also bring major new industries, ones that either do not yet exist or that are just beginning. Wind electricity generation is one such industry. Now in its embryonic stage, it promises to become the foundation of the new energy economy. In effect, there will be three new subsidiary industries associated with wind power: turbine manufacturing, installation, and maintenance. Manufacturing facilities will be found in scores of countries, industrial and developing. Installation, which is basically a construction industry, will be more local in nature. Maintenance, since it is a day-to-day activity, will be a source of ongoing local employment.

Training Personnel for a New Economic System The Church already owns scores of educational institutions. If we have a vision about a new society emerging, then we should start institutions to train the personnel for the new economy. "And it shall come to pass afterward, that I will pour out my spirit on all flesh; your sons and your daughters shall prophesy, your old men shall dream dreams, and your young men shall see visions" (Joel 2:28). It is true that Church could not bring out such a new economic order which has political, economic, social, and other dimensions. Church should facilitate an ecological vision of the new society to emerge. A prophetic Church should foresee such changes i.e expanding professions in an eco-friendly economy. This will be a catalytic work for building up a new economy. Here the role of the Church is the role of a midwife. Lester R Brown in his book Eco-Economics mentions some of the job opportunities available in the new economic order.

Wind Meteorologists As wind becomes an increasingly prominent energy source, there will be a need for thousands of wind meteorologists to analyse potential wind sites, monitor wind speeds, and select the best sites for wind farms. The better the data on wind resources, the more efficient the industry will become. Wind meteorologists will play a role in the new energy economy comparable to that of petroleum geologists in the old one. Worldwide, the use of wind power alone has multiplied nearly fourfold over the last five years, a growth rate matched only by the computer industry. Closely related to this new profession will be the wind engineers who design the wind turbines. Again, the appropriate turbine size and design can vary widely according to the site. It will be the job of wind engineers to tailor designs to specific wind regimes in order to maximise electricity generation.

Family Planning Midwives If the world population is to stabilise soon, literally millions of family planning midwives will be required.

Foresters Reforesting the earth will require professional guidance on what species to plant where and in what combination.

Hydrologists In a future of water scarcity, watershed hydrologists will be in demand. It will be their responsibility to understand the hydrological cycle, including the movement of underground water, and to know the depth of aquifers and determine their sustainable yield. They will be at the center of watershed management regimes. As water scarcity spreads, the demand for hydrologists to advise on watershed management, water sources, and water efficiency will increase.

Aqua-cultural Veterinarians Until now, veterinarians have typically specialised in either large animals or small animals, but with fish farming likely to overtake beef production before the end of this decade, marine veterinarians will be in demand.

Ecological Economists As it becomes clear that the basic principles of ecology must be incorporated into economic planning and policymaking, the demand for economists able to think like ecologists will grow.

Geothermal Geologists With the likelihood that large areas of the world will turn to geothermal energy both for electricity and for heating, the demand for geothermal geologists will increase.

Environmental Architects Architects are learning the principles of ecology so that they can incorporate them into the buildings in which we live and work. Environmental architecture is another fast-growing profession. Among the signposts of an environmentally sustainable economy are buildings that are in harmony with the environment. Environmental architects design buildings that are energy- and materials-efficient and that maximise natural heating, cooling, and lighting.

Bicycle Mechanics As the world turns to the bicycle for transportation and exercise, bicycle mechanics will be needed to keep the fleet running.

Wind Turbine Engineers With millions of wind turbines likely to be installed in the decades ahead, there will be strong worldwide demand for wind turbine engineers.

Sanitary Engineers Another pressing need, particularly in developing countries, is for sanitary engineers who can design sewage systems not dependent on water, a trend that is already under way in some water-scarce countries.

Technologists for Hydrogen Generation As the transition from a carbon-based to a hydrogen-based energy economy progresses, hydrogen generation will become a huge industry as hydrogen replaces coal and oil.

Fuel Cell Manufacturing Technician As fuel cells replace internal combustion engines in automobiles and begin generating power in buildings, a huge market will evolve.

Solar Cell Manufacturing Technician For many of the 2 billion people living in rural third world communities who lack electricity, solar cells will be the best bet for electrification.

Light Rail Construction As people tire of the traffic congestion and pollution associated with the automobile, cities in industrial and developing countries alike will be turning to light rail to provide mobility.

Comprehensive Re-cycling Technologists As efforts to close the materials cycle intensify, many throwaway products will be either banned or taxed out of existence. As the world shifts from a throwaway economy, engineers will be needed to design products that can be recycled—from cars to computers. Once products are designed to be disassembled quickly and easily into component parts and materials, comprehensive re-cycling is relatively easy.

Teleconferencing Another industry that will play a prominent role in the new economy, one that will reduce energy use, is teleconferencing. Increasingly for environmental reasons and to save time, individuals will be "attending" conferences electronically with both audio and visual connections. This industry involves developing the electronic global infrastructure, as well as the services, to make this possible. One day there will likely be literally thousands of firms organizing electronic conferences. Restructuring the global economy will create not only new industries, but also new jobs—indeed, whole new professions and new specialities within professions.

Restructuring the Economy These aspects give us some idea of the size of the ecological crisis of the planetary system. The earth is sick and wounded. Human beings, especially with the advent of the industrial revolution, have proved that they are exterminating angels and veritable demons of the earth. But human beings could also become guardian angels, intent upon saving the earth, which is fatherland and motherland. What kind of society do we want? Surely we want it to be more participatory, egalitarian, aiming at solidarity, and capable of uniting imagination and analytical reason. The world energy economy is on the verge of a major transformation. Historically, the twentieth century was the century of fossil fuels. Coal, already well established as a major fuel source in 1900, was joined by oil when the automobile came on the scene. It was not until 1967, however, that oil finally replaced coal as the workhorse of the world energy economy. Natural gas moved ahead of coal in 1999 gaining in popularity during the closing decades of the last century as concern about urban air pollution and global climate change escalated. We know the kind of restructuring that is needed. In simplest terms, our fossil-fuel-based, automobile-centered, throwaway economy is not a viable model for the world. According to Lester R Brown, the alternative is a solar/hydrogen energy economy, an urban transport system that is centred on advanced-design public rail systems and that relies more on the bicycle and less on the automobile, and a comprehensive reuse/recycle economy. Alongside all of this we need to stabilise population as soon as possible.

Conclusion We believe that God loves creation and wants its life to flourish. No creature is different in God's sight. Every creature has its own dignity and its own rights, because all are included in God's covenant. So it is said in the story of Noah: "Behold", says God, " I establish my covenant with you and your descendants after you, and every living creature" (Gen 9: 9-10). The fundamental human rights come from this covenant "with us". The rights of future generations come from the covenant "with us and our descendants." The rights of nature come from the covenant "with us and our descendants and with every living creature". Before God, the creator, we and our descendants and every living creature are equal partners of God's covenant. Nature is not our property. ALL Living beings must be respected by humanity as God's partners in the covenant. Whoever destroys nature, destroys him/herself. Whoever injures the dignity of the animals, injures God. We should consider earth as a single complex system, as a living organism. Every subsystem is linked to all other subsystems through the blowing of the winds, the oceans, the migration of species, the cycles of growth, maturation, ageing and death. By means of the air that we breathe we are united with all animals, all plants, but also our vehicles, factories, and all our industrial chimneys. Hence we have to build an economy that will support, not undermine, future generations. As an organized body, Church can work as a catalyst in this transformation for a sustainable economy. Green Church movements are for building up a sustainable economy to protect the rights of future generations.

## References

Eco-Economy, Lester R Brown, (2002), Orient Longman.

Cross-cultural Eco theology in an Indian Ocean Context. Edited by Chilkuri Vasantha Rao, David Richardt, ISPCK (2018).

Ahead of Nature, Dileep Kulkarni, (1998), Vivekananda Kendra Prakashan Trust.

Planetwise, Davebookless (2008), Intervarsity Press.

9

# A Liturgy Towards Hospitality:
## Liturgical Perspectives on Borderless Church

**Viji Varghese Eapen**

I begin this article stating how "liturgy towards hospitality" differs from the "liturgy of hospitality" or "liturgical hospitality". The "liturgy of hospitality" refers to worship, where everyone irrespective of their distinct identities and differences is welcomed. Almost all ecumenical liturgies, for example, the Church of South India liturgy which embraces the Western (Anglican, Congregationalist, Methodist and Presbyterian) as well as Eastern (Saint James Liturgy) theological and liturgical perspectives, follow this pattern of the "liturgy of hospitality". However, a "liturgy towards hospitality" deliberates not only about making the liturgy relevant to the worshipping community but also explores the possibility of such a liturgy nourishing the Church to be truly ecumenical, or in other words, "borderless". The Church of South India Eucharist Liturgy (revised in 2006) which includes three alternatives for the prayer of "Great Thanksgiving" – traditional, liberation and ecological perspectives – has qualities of a "liturgy towards hospitality", and provides directions concerning how the Church of South India (CSI) aspires to become a borderless Church, an all-embracing and non-exclusive community.[1]

## Liturgy for a Borderless Church: From Rights to Responsibilities

Ever since the discussions regarding a "Borderless Church" had begun, there have been attempts to explore its implications upon ecclesiology, ecumenism, diaconia and liturgy of the Church, using theological, Christological, Pneumatological and Trinitarian approaches. For the CSI, regardless of these approaches, borderlessness was about rediscovering the essence of being and becoming a Christ Community. In his "Concept Note" regarding the borderless church, Daniel Ratnakara Sadananda (CSI General Secretary during 2014 - 2020) mentions some of the features of this border-less-ness distinctive to the first century Christ communities.

> The early Church was indeed borderless, as it understood Jesus' command to go and make disciples of all nations (Matt.28:19), as a mandate to create borderless Christ communities. It also had a clear geographical strategy, 'you will be witnesses, in Jerusalem and in all Judea and Samaria and to the ends of the earth' (Acts 1:8). Peter also is 'converted' to the borderless Church, after the vision and reality experience at Joppa and Caesarea. Paul, after his world-encircling, missional engagements, writes his faith conviction; his magna carta "there is neither Jew nor Greek Slave nor free, male or female for you are all one in Christ" (Gal.3:28). It is very consistent with his sacramental theology which envisions a borderless church, "Do you not know that all of us who have been baptized into Christ Jesus were baptized into his death? Therefore, we have been buried with him by baptism into death, so that, just as Christ was raised from the dead by the glory of the Father, so we too might walk in newness of life." (Rom.6:3, 4). Every follower of Christ has been baptized into Christ, and therefore when Paul writes to Corinthians he clarifies that "The bread that we break, is it not a sharing in the body of Christ? Because there is one bread, we who are many are one body, for we all partake of the one bread." (1 Cor.10:16, 17) [2]

The word "liturgy" (derived from "leitos", meaning "people" and "ergos", meaning work) refers more to our praxis (actions), whether of an individual or a community. In other words, liturgy, more than a plethora of prayers, rites and rituals, engaged at a set-apart sacred space, refers to our practical way of living well with God and to the rest of His creation, as a "sacred-secular" expression.[3] About liturgy and ethics, Paul Ramsey says, '*Lex orandi lex credendi lex bene operandi.* The order of prayer is the order of believing is the order of doing well'.[4] Further, he adds that in any combination of these three activities of the Church, praying, believing and well-doing, no subordination should be implied of one or two of these actions to a third. Along these lines, the liturgy towards hospitality is a clarion call for the Church to allow divine interference to transform our ethical actions through our liturgical actions towards rethinking the ecclesia to become borderless. Therefore, to worship is a political act as what we pray, what we believe, and what we act correspond to the politics of Jesus. It intensifies the Church towards being and becoming a borderless community, where hospitality serves as the central theme.

However, the border-less-ness referred here is not about the absence of borders. Cláudio Carvalhaes, narrating his experience as a Pastor, of being challenged constantly to offer hospitality (which he calls as "Eucharistic Hospitality"), to people at the doors of two small churches, Santa Fe and Fall River, with whom he had neither connections nor anything in common, refers to several 'blurred, complicated and interconnected borders' such as ecclesiastical, theological, liturgical and social/economic borders where liturgical practices and spaces must engage and be engaged.'[5] He says that these borders serve as separation as well as protection.

> Borders are everywhere. Every border regulates and contains and excludes. Borders are a controlling apparatus, concrete and symbolic, real and imaginary, paradoxical and determined, entangling space and power within various other areas such as knowledge, identities, politics, economics. Borders also mark spaces: margins, frontiers, hinges, lines and thresholds in constant relation with something else, separating, marking space and differing positions. Borders, controlled from the inside, keep out everything that cannot be accepted, invited and lived. Borders, controlled from the inside, keep out everything that cannot be accepted, invited and lived.

> The various degrees of invitation entail categories of participation according to some chosen criteria. Some will be invited as short term guests, others as distinguished guests, others as a long term guests, and so on. Borders also serve as signs of protection, safety, and order. They convey stability, permanence and duration. On the other hand, this protection and stability demand that those who are inside do not challenge the authenticity of the borders.[6]

However, he says, despite the concept of protection and separation, the borders are made of a porous structure with unattended spaces. Onora Sylvia O'Neill, who has written widely on political philosophy and ethics, international justice, bioethics and the philosophy of Immanuel Kant, in her article, 'Distant Strangers, Moral Standing and Porous Boundaries', refers to such porous boundaries from geographical and political perspectives. She differentiates between the "cosmopolitans" who advocate for a porous state boundary, and the "communitarians" who demand an impervious state boundary[7]. Although she supports the concept of porous boundaries of the cosmopolitans, warns about the risks in the total abolition of boundaries, and advocates for "just and porous boundaries". Such a "moral cosmopolitanism", prioritising obligations rather than rights as fundamental to distant strangers as well as those near at hand, calls not for the abolition of state boundaries creating a stateless world, but for just and porous state boundaries.[8] A just and porous state boundary treats strangers justly, either by transforming the boundaries of exclusion into porous boundaries or by compensating the strangers for negative impacts of unjustifiable exclusions upon them.

Therefore, the concept of border-less-ness as "just and porous borders" is possible only when we shift our focus from rights to responsibilities. O'Neill argues the significance of obligations or responsibilities in affording a more consistent and complete starting point for reasoning about ethical requirements.

> There are reasons enough to that obligations provide the more coherent and more comprehensive starting point for thinking about ethical requirements, including the requirements of justice.

> Although the rhetoric of rights has a heady power, and that of obligations and duties few immediate attractions, it helps to view the perspective of obligations as fundamental if the political and ethical implications of normative claims are to be taken seriously. [...] Even if we have reasons to think that each individual has certain rights, this alone will not be enough to establish who must act, or from each right-holder might rightfully claim particular rights. However, if we can establish some principles of justice, and have at least a practical account of the scope of moral concern, then we may be able to start by identifying what is required in order to work towards just institutions.[9]

Although O'Neill applies the framework of responsibilities rather than rights to elaborate upon her theme of justice-based porous borders, this article adopts the same structure to develop the concept of a hospitality-based border-less-ness. A Church that aspires to be borderless should consider hospitality not as a category of right but responsibility in its order of prayer, the order of believing and the order of doing. In other words, a paradigm shift from a liturgy that adjusts on rights, to a liturgy that insists on responsibility, particularly towards promoting the culture and politics of hospitality, is crucial to the being and becoming of a borderless Church.

## Rethinking Ecclesia: Liturgical Perspectives based on Hospitality

In the 'Parable of the Good Samaritan', there is a priest, a Levite, and a Samaritan who encounters a wounded stranger on the route from Jerusalem to Jericho. The parable is told by Jesus, addressing a lawyer's question based on his "right-consciousness" about eternal life. However, Jesus, through this parable, shifts the focus from rights to responsibility, from law to love, and from the "divine" to the "mundane", emphasising upon the vital concept of hospitality to strangers. Often, considering the priest and the Levite as belonging to a liturgical class, while the Good Samaritan belonging to a non-liturgical category, it is often interpreted that it was because of their liturgical responsibilities that the priest and the Levite had failed to attend to the wounded stranger.

In other words, they are believed to have overlooked their "*lex bene operandi*", because of their "*lex orandii*" and " *lex credenda*". Their liturgical commitment appears to have required them to circumvent their ethical requirement.

However, an exegesis of the text reveals that the reason for them, especially the priest, bypassing the wounded man was not their (his) busy liturgical responsibility. Luke 10: 31 reads, '[...] a priest was going down that road'. The Greek word used for "going down" is "κατέβαινεν" which means "to descend", and it implies a movement downwards, from Jerusalem Temple, which was situated higher, to Jericho, a valley. Therefore, the priest, and probably the Levite also, were travelling not to the temple, instead, from the temple, after completing their liturgical roles. Thus, what stops them from helping the man lying on the road was not any urgent liturgical commitment; instead, their apathy and indifference. Jesus mentions that both the priest and the Levite consciously and deliberately passed by the other side (Greek "ἀντιπαρῆλθεν" = pass by the opposite side). Their repulsive thought that any contact with the man, who looked dead, would ceremonially defile them, might have caused their apathy. Hence, their liturgical role does not motivate them to engage in an ethical act. They are unable to engage in an expression of border-less-ness, since they are conscious only about their right for purity, and not about their responsibility towards charity.

On the other hand, the Samaritan saw the man lying on the road and reached out to him, despite the hostility between the Jews and Samaritans. Samaritans were despised and rejected by the Jews as they were a mixed-blood race with the mixed religious system of beliefs. Nevertheless, he could transcend the hostility with the Jews through his act of hospitality. Apart from their medicinal value, both oil and wine have liturgical and sacramental significance. Hence, the Samaritan becomes the "priest", the way-side becomes the "altar", and the act of hospitality becomes the worship. Most importantly, the

Samaritan himself becomes the sacrament of the divine grace. In other words, Jesus is trying to teach the lawyer that being and becoming a borderless neighbour, in whom liturgy and ethics unite to engage in the act of hospitality, are essential to aspire for eternity.

A relevant liturgy for a borderless Church, *firstly*, ought to be a liturgy that focuses more on responsibility than right, that encourages the Church to found on hospitality than hostility, and that looks beyond the rites and rituals to ethics and morality in the sacred as well as secular space. For Carvalhaes, to create such a hospitable liturgy is 'a theological Sisyphean task of creating, relocating, connecting and dismantling borders'.[10] He says that as we gather at the table, we also prepare the way to share with our neighbours who might have nothing in common with us. Ultimately all borders are crossed and exchanged so that worship becomes 'challenging, offensive and healing, stretching and transformative'.

> As we gather 'with' one another we must prepare the tables and altars as we 'prepare the way' for our neighbors and for the world: hearts, spaces, food, minds and bodies ready for communion with somebody else. There we share what cannot be shared and commune with those who might have nothing in common with us. There, the Christian worship might be festive and challenging, offensive and healing, stretching and transformative. Together, with little or nothing in common, we pray and sing, and walk and talk, and believe and lose our beliefs; we understand and have no idea, and we practice with one another what we have received from traditions and that which we invent and add to the traditions.[11]

*Secondly*, as David Tracy says about theology as a public discourse, that "speak from and to three publics: society, academy and church', liturgy also should become a public discourse.[12] Such a liturgy will take the form of a 'public liturgy', which as James Newman says about a "public church", will not 'stand apart from the wounds of our world but fully shares that plight to bring an alternative word of lasting life.'[13] It will dialectically engage theology and experiences of the marginalised communities, expressed in their culture, for example, public rituals of invoking divine power to restore the wellbeing of the ruptured community and out of sync natural order; communal rituals of confession and repentance before the Divine and each other; sacrificial rituals for the release of inauspiciousness spirits and restoration of auspicious powers for the life of the community; and collective celebration of hope in a new alignment between the Divine, human beings, and the cosmic order to usher wellbeing for all. As Carvalhaes observes, by creating such a variety of liturgies,

> [...] we might be able to open up gestures, movements, practices and various performances that might help us expand the borders of our own comprehension of the sacrament and perhaps, only perhaps, foster a radical theology of hospitality that might take the stranger and the poor into greater consideration, even at the risk of losing one's own place at the table.[14]

*Finally*, a liturgy towards hospitality transcends (but includes) *liturgia* (liturgy) as *logoi* (words). Liturgy as words, and connected signs and symbols, continue to express, determine, direct and transform our moral thoughts and ethical actions. However, more than that, it calls to consider our secular ethical contexts as sacred spaces to enact liturgy by obliterating borders between our liturgical and ethical actions. This also brings to question the epistemology of a borderless liturgy which cannot be limited to the sacred space. In other words, such a liturgy would challenge the hierarchy of knowledge: the dominance of the sacred knowledge, taken to be eternally true, over the mundane knowledge, considered to be 'obvious, transient, low in or devoid of sanctity, and continent or instrumental rather than fundamental.'[15]

The mundane experience of the migrants, refugees, victims of caste and class discrimination, women, children, people of all faiths and of no faith, of all minorities and vulnerable communities, count to contribute to its borderless epistemology. For this, as George Zachariah proposes, our ecclesiological and liturgical discourses should shift from considering Church as a 'house' where practices of exclusion provide its identity, to Church as an 'event', whose identity is derived from the expressions of hospitality such as fellowship, solidarity, compassion etc..

> The identity of the house is determined by the fortified walls that keep the Other away from it. Said differently, it is our practices of exclusion which provide the house its identity. So house is a symbol of exclusion. Our supremacy and honor are mediated through our practices of exclusion which discursively constructs the Other as impure, shameful, and inferior. In contrast to this familiar, dominant, and comfortable model of house, I would like to propose a different model for the Church. Church is not a monument that is built on the foundations of traditions and doctrines; rather it is an empowering and transforming experience that happens in the lives of the communities on the margins. Here Church becomes an event. Church happens as fellowship, solidarity, love, care, compassion, justice, and restoration in the lives of people, who go through the tragic experience of utter God-forsakenness.[16]

## Conclusion

Borderlessness is about rediscovering the essence of being and becoming a Christ Community. For such an ecclesiology, as well as liturgy, the concept of hospitality is crucial. A "liturgy towards hospitality", on the one hand, deliberates to make the liturgy relevant to the worshipping community, while on the other hand, explores the possibility of such a liturgy nourishing the Church to be borderless. Firstly, such a liturgy, instead of adjusting on rights, shall insist on responsibility, particularly towards promoting the culture and politics of hospitality. Secondly, it shall take the form of a public liturgy that dialectically engages theology and experiences of the marginalised communities, expressed in their culture. Lastly, it shall challenge the hierarchy of knowledge: the dominance of the sacred knowledge over the mundane knowledge.

## Endnotes

[1] [...] the prayer of *Great Thanksgiving* in *the Breaking of the Bread* has three alternatives: the first one interprets the salvation history and the Christ event using the traditional concepts of ransom and propitiation, the second alternative celebrates the salvation drama from the liberation perspective,

and the third one looks at it from a creational point of view. ['Preamble', in *The Church of South India Book of Common Worship* (Chennai: Church of South India, 2006), pp. ix-xvi (p. xii).]

[2] Daniel Ratnakara Sadananda, 'Towards a Borderless Church' (presented at the Rethinking Ecclesia, Chennai, 2018), pp. 1–4.

[3] This article considers "sacred" and "secular" not as antonyms, but two spaces engaged in a dialectical relation to enhancing our moral and ethical life.

[4] Paul Ramsey, 'Liturgy and Ethics', *The Journal of Religious Ethics*, 7.2 (1979), 139–71 (p. 139).

[5] The Eucharist can help us with ways to understand these borders and ways Christian hospitality might be (un)framed. At the eucharistic table, one is able to describe the ways in which Christian hospitality is understood, presented and performed. At the same place, one also sees ecclesiastical borders, which delimit the ways a community defines who is in and who is out, and determines the norms and standards of its identity; theological borders, which give content to the ecclesiastical borders and ensure that liturgical procedures are correctly done and expressed in obedience and faith to God; liturgical borders, which limit and locate the liminal space, giving contours (and content in their own way) to the theological and ecclesiastical borders, depicting a proper language, bodily gestures and ritual actions to make the rite right and familiar; social/economic borders, which define the sacred spaces where social classes attest how God acts and who belongs there; and political borders, which show that the limits of eucharistic hospitality have to do with political choices and allegiances, economic commitments and social engagements. [Cláudio Carvalhaes, 'Borders, Globalization and Eucharistic Hospitality', *Dialog*, 49.1 (2010), 45–55 (p. 45).]

[6] Carvalhaes, 'Borders, Globalization and Eucharistic Hospitality' (p. 47).

[7] Onora O'Neill, 'Distance Strangers, Moral Standing and Porous Boundaries', in *Bounds of Justice* (Cambridge: Cambridge University Press, 2000), pp. 186–202 (pp. 188-189).

[8] O'Neill, 'Distance Strangers, Moral Standing and Porous Boundaries' (pp. 198-200).

[9] O'Neill, 'Distance Strangers, Moral Standing and Porous Boundaries' (p. 199).

[10] Carvalhaes, 'Borders, Globalization and Eucharistic Hospitality' (p. 52).

[11] Carvalhaes, 'Borders, Globalization and Eucharistic Hospitality'.

[12] David Tracy, *The Analogical Imagination: Christian Theology and the Culture of Pluralism* (New York: Crossroad, 1981), p. 264.

[13] James Neiman, 'Centrifugal: Being a Public Church', *Living Lutheran*, 2016 <https://www.livinglutheran.org/2016/06/centrifugal-public-church/> [accessed 30 April 2018].

[14] Carvalhaes, 'Borders, Globalization and Eucharistic Hospitality' (p. 54).

[15] Roy A. Rappaport, *Ritual and Religion in the Making of Humanity* (Cambridge: Cambridge University Press, 1999), p. 450.

[16] George Zachariah, 'Church: A Rainbow Community of Hospitality, Fellowship and Solidarity' <https://www.academia.edu/6774394/Church_A_Rainbow_Community_of_Hospitality_Fellowship_and_Solidarity> [accessed 16 April 2020].

## Bibliography

Carvalhaes, Cláudio, 'Borders, Globalization and Eucharistic Hospitality', *Dialog*, 49.1 (2010), 45–55

Neiman, James, 'Centrifugal: Being a Public Church', *Living Lutheran*, 2016 <https://www.livinglutheran.org/2016/06/centrifugal-public-church/> [accessed 31 October 2019]

O'Neill, Onora, 'Distance Strangers, Moral Standing and Porous Boundaries', in *Bounds of Justice* (Cambridge: Cambridge University Press, 2000), pp. 186–202

Ramsey, Paul, 'Liturgy and Ethics', *The Journal of Religious Ethics*, 7.2 (1979), 139–71

Rappaport, Roy A., *Ritual and Religion in the Making of Humanity* (Cambridge: Cambridge University Press, 1999)

Sadananda, Daniel Ratnakara, 'Towards a Borderless Church' (presented at the Rethinking Ecclesia, Chennai, 2018), pp. 1–4

*The Church of South India Book of Common Worship* (Chennai: Church of South India, 2006)

Tracy, David, *The Analogical Imagination: Christian Theology and the Culture of Pluralism* (New York: Crossroad, 1981)

Zachariah, George, 'Church: A Rainbow Community of Hospitality, Fellowship and Solidarity' <https://www.academia.edu/6774394/Church_A_Rainbow_Community_of_Hospitality_Fellowship_and_Solidarity> [accessed 16 April 2020]

10

# Liturgy and the Borderless Church

**Jyoti Isaac**

Both "liturgy" and "borderless Church" do not have clear cut definitions and therefore are hard to explain. Scholars do not seem to have a consensus on what is meant by the English word liturgy especially when it is related to the word worship. Liturgy is a term used with different connotations by different people of different denominations at different periods. We may even say that it is a term which is in the processes of attaining its full and correct meaning. According to Dom Gregory Dix "'The Liturgy' is the term which covers generally all that is worship which is officially organized by the church, and which is open to and offered by, or in the name of, all who are members of the church." Lowther Clarke in his introduction to the book, *Liturgy and Worship*, tries to explain the difference between worship and liturgy, but with a question mark to ask if "Worship (is) the inner movement of the soul of which liturgy is the outward manifestation?" Michael Perham says, "Worship and liturgy are not exactly the same thing." He further states, "Liturgy is that subtle blend of word, song, movement, gesture and silence that enables the people of God to worship together."

The opinions of these three scholars themselves differ in their connotations. For Gregory Dix, liturgy is worship, but officially arranged by the church. For the other two, there are some differences between the two words, and from their definitions it can be understood that liturgy is the order or programme of an act of worship. M.M. Schaefer maintains almost the same view. To him, "The term liturgy refers especially to those forms of public corporate worship which follow a set structure or series of rites (procedures required or usual in a solemn celebration). The specific form or formularies used in public worship are also designated as liturgy."

In my opinion, the views of these scholars are suitable for this study. Hence, in this presentation, I use the term liturgy in the sense of an order of worship service.

## Borderless Church

"Borderless church" is a vision undergoing widespread discussions as part of ecumenism. So far, its final and perfect form has not yet developed. The extent of a borderless church is to be defined. Do the border extends up to the boundaries of Christian world, irrespective of denominations, or does it go beyond? In its literal sense, doe it include all people, irrespective of religion? Let us try to understand the vision of the borderless church in its literal meaning for our study. Let us bring to mind the vision put forward by the Rev. Dr. D. Retnakara Sadananda, the General Secretary of the CSI is his concept note for this consultation, "... a borderless Church travels beyond suspicion, fear and hostility in a multi-religious, multilingual, multicultural society."

## Liturgy and Borderless Church

While we think about a Christian liturgy in relation to a borderless church, what are the things we have to consider especially from the CSI point of view? Up to what extent can we go? Can we make changes in our liturgy, just to make it acceptable to all people? What are the fields we have to cover? Is liturgy necessary for a borderless church?

## Need for Liturgy

"Let all things be done decently and in order" (1 Cor 14:40). Christian worship is an activity of a community so some guiding factors to maintain order and quality are needed, as without this worship will seem a mess. Liturgy is this guiding factor for a worship service which is, in fact, the body of the worship. From the very beginning the Church insisted on an order in worship services. That is what we see in the advice of Paul to the Corinthians. To safeguard this decency and order, an order of service or liturgy is necessary. Moreover, a liturgy reveals the theological conviction and identity of a church.

## The Phenomenon of Worship

Worship is one of the oldest social activities of humanity, irrespective of country, culture and creed, which is the most suitable and direct way to express human regard and gratitude to God in his presence. "Worship is a universal phenomenon. It consists of a response of veneration in the face of the recognized presence of God." According to Evelyn Underhil, "Worship, in all its grades and kinds, is the response of the creature to the eternal; nor need we limit this definition to the human sphere."

As mentioned in the foreword to the Book of Common Worship, published by the CSI, "Worship forms the epicenter of every faith community. All that a faith community is and does is rooted in and moulded through its worship." Worship is like a celebration of a family fellowship in which all the members of the family who live at different places gather together and encircle around their father, who is at the centre. As J.D.Crichton says, "Worship … is the privileged moment (kairos) where we can meet both God and man." Worship binds both the community and God together. Since worship is the meeting point of God and man (worshipper), naturally they are the main parties in it.

## Christian Worship

Christian worship is, in essence an act of the Church that signifies the following:

1. An act of accepting God – his existence, authority, sovereignty, power and glory.
2. An act of reverencing God – blessing, praising and glorifying.
3. An act of thanks giving to God – for his act of salvation, providence and love.
4. An act of humbling before God – realizing our weakness and limitations.
5. An act of responding to God's call – his parental call for fellowship.
6. An act of fellowship with God and fellow beings – as a family with their father.
7. An act of listening to God – moments of silence to hear God's voice of consolation, empowering and challenging.
8. An act of submitting to God – to his will and to his orders, and committing to fulfill them.
9. An act of receiving God's blessings – being empowered to face life with hope and confidence.
10. An act of equipping for further life – being sent to society with vision, commitment and strength to do our duties well.

Worship helps to build up awareness of God and of a social commitment among people. In worship both God's existence and human experience of God are regenerated and remembered. Worship is not a one sided act, but a mutual act by God and people. "Because it is God who always takes the initiative, Christian worship is best discussed in the terms of response." The dependence on God and the belief that he cares for us creates a strong relationship with God and it empowers the worshipper for day-to-day life and work.

## Dual Dimension of Worship

The basic character of Christian worship is its synergetic dual dimension, i.e. God-centered and people-oriented. The history of Christian liturgy is in fact the history of the way in which this basic character is maintained. Though the main focus of worship is God, the worshipper is an important factor for its fulfillment. In worship we expect not only the presence of God, but also that of people. Therefore worship should be capable of ensuring achievement of these two goals. The sound of worship should be audible, sensible and pleasing to both parties.

In the Apostolic age when Christian liturgy began to take shape this dual dimension was the warp and weft of the fabric of worship (Acts 2:46; 4.24, 31-33; 12.5, 12). In the patristic period this healthy alignment was safeguarded in worship but in the medieval period there began a change. The participation of the people of God in worship of God began to lose its importance and they were separated from God's presence by "curtain, screen or even wall". In J.D. Crichton's opinion, "The Mass-liturgy of the last eight or nine centuries has, of course, driven the laity to this attitude, for it was a liturgy that they could only see (though not always) and hear (though again not always) and in which their own activity was reduced to walking to the alter rails for communion." This separation of people from worship resulted in their alienation from Christian faith and growth of atheistic ideologies.

Christian worship is a life long spiritual learning journey – from birth to death. In this life long journey a person learns Christian life, worship, spirituality, morality, ethics, values and so on. Each act of worship should be capable of educating people of all ages to equip them further to worship God in the most appropriate way, and to grow in relationship with him in Christ.

## Decline in People's Participation in Worship

One of the major issues that face the Church today is the decline of people's participation in worship services. As J.D. Crichton says, "A fact of our time is the mass abandonment of regular Sunday worship." The graveness of the issue can be understood from the fact that, in the west, many large Churches were closed due to lack of people's attendance, and many are on the verge of closing. As a very serious issue it needs a deep and detailed study.

Churches are seriously thinking about this crisis and doing many things to solve it. The recent attempts, in applying many new techniques and tactics in worship to attract people and make it more successful is part of this. In such a move, generally, the taste and liking of the worshipper gets more consideration. Some people say such liturgies are "too human-centered." Here arise a few questions:

1. Who is the centre of worship – God or man?
2. Can there be two different centers in worship?
3. Can there be anything as human-centered worship?

## Centre of Worship

When we think about worship, the central figure which naturally comes to our mind is God. The foreword of the *Book of Common Worship*, published by the CSI is clearly mentioned that, "Worship is an act of ascribing supreme worth to God, our creator, Redeemer and Sustainer." From the origin of liturgy God was its centre. To safeguard this focus in worship people were taught about God, the need for worshipping him, the proper way of worship and so on. The Bible can be said to be such a text book. There are occasions when even God himself instructed his people about these things. The opening books of the Bible beginning from Exodus are good examples of this (Exod 19-31; Lev 1- 8:3; 10:8- 11:22; 17-27). There is no doubt about the centre of worship – it is God. And it is unnatural to think about two centers in worship. Hence saying that worship is "too human-centered" is absurd. Something "human-centered" cannot be a worship of God.

However, as already mentioned, as an integral partner, the worshipper is an important factor in worship, and his interests should be safeguarded in it, but not at the cost of losing God's centrality. How can worship be arranged attractively and enjoyably for the worshipper at the same time as keeping it God-centered and spiritual? Balancing this dual dimension is a most important and delicate task, and it is one of the main concerns of liturgists and leaders of worship.

## Remedial Measures Taken

The modern period has witnessed some good attempts to rectify errors and to regain the lost balance of worship. The liturgical movement and the reforms that it entailed, preceded by the Reformation and Counter Reformation, can be cited as examples. A reformed outlook is visible in the new liturgies which aimed at making a prophetic Church. According to Roger Haight, "The liturgies symbolize the priority of God's love and forgiveness; they also provide a stimulus or challenge in leading the Christian life." There was an international step to make liturgy as a strengthening means to lead to a grace inspired life in the world. "By creating worship that is 'authentic' and that enables a full-orbed exposure to the transforming power of Christ in the spirit, the people of God are to be motivated and equipped to serve him in the world." A dualistic vision of a grace-filled church and a grace-devoid world is not the goal. "Rather, in the liturgy the grace of the world becomes conscious in memory and promise in order that it may become intensified in daily life."

In Monika K Hellwig's opinion, "The most obvious shift in the way in which the Church exists and functions since the second Vatican council is the move from being a heavily clerical to an actively lay Church." There was a conscious move to restore the community nature of worship. "Worship is no longer a spectacle but a community action

– a shift which leads to the discovery of the potentially cohesive power of ritual and ceremony." More importance was given to vernacular language in worship which enabled people to participate in it with understanding.

## Some Issues to Be Addressed in Liturgy

While the liturgical movement and liturgical reforms were initiated by scholars, a parallel movement was started by people who were not theologically oriented and who gave importance to the emotional side of worship. Their only aim is to attract and gather people at any cost. For that the worship is arranged in a way to make people happy. Fast rhythm music and a highly advanced sound system are the main attraction of such gatherings. In such gatherings it is difficult to find the proper place of God, especially in the context of worship. An observation by one National English daily, *The Hindu*, is noteworthy. As it observes, a number of groups, known as "Independent Churches", have mushroomed in Kerala, one of the southern states of India. "There is music, fast rhythm, touching songs, accompanied by a lot of body movements. One member said it was as exciting as attending a rock concert…." (*The Hindu* dated 17-06-2002). Is this experience the goal of worship?

A few questions are to be raised here:

1. How long can people be retained in the church by giving the enjoyment of the world? Will they not go for the original source?
2. How will this phenomenon affect the life of the people?
3. How will it affect the very nature of the church, the body of Christ?

Now some mainline Churches too try to imitate such techniques as they see larger gatherings in Independent Churches. At present an imbalance in the dual dimension of worship is seen in many services. In some places the importance of God is ignored, and in some other places that of people. In both cases the purpose of worship is not served. It is difficult to see the right balance of the vertical (towards God) and the horizontal (towards co-worshippers) relationship, both of which have to be maintained in worship. How can this ideal relationship be maintained properly?

## Conclusion

While we discuss the subject, "Liturgy and the borderless church" in a multi-religious, multilingual, multicultural context, we have to be very careful, cautious and conscious about the consequences. An earnest attempt to bring back the synergetic dual dimension of worship, i.e. God-centered and people-oriented, is necessary. Liturgy should be understandable, sensible, pleasing and acceptable for the society which is multi-religious, multilingual and multicultural. We cannot make any compromise in the basic truths and principles of Christian liturgy, which we received from the scripture. At the same time the language, terminologies and the cultural background of the worshippers are also to be considered. A liturgy which is totally foreign for a society in language, terminology and culture will not be meaningful.

11

# Rethinking Ecclesia: Towards Being and Becoming Christ Communities – A Borderless Church from a Prophetic Diakonia Persepective[1]

**S. Samuel Rajadurai**

## 1. INTRODUCTION

The Church is critically evaluating itself, assessing its life and work, from time to time. Through this study programme, the Church of South India is estimating its identity and relevance in the present context. The faith community made many changes in its comprehension and conclusion on various issues over the years. The relationship with people of other faith is one among them. On the one hand it said,"Do not be mismatched with unbelievers. For what partnership is there between righteousness and lawlessness? Or what fellowship is there between light and darkness?"(Cf 2 Cor 6:14).On the other hand the Jerusalem council broke the barriers of Torah and reached for the people outside the law for the fellowship of the early church (Cf. Acts 15:19).

The sacraments of the church were ordained to surpass all the borders created by the world and to facilitate union. However as years pass by, they were used to form borders that divide people. At the same time the life-world in which we exist and have our being, group up the human community on various categories like Rotary club, trade union, fans association, residents of a colony, etc., transcending the borders created by caste, class, ethnicity, language, religion, and the like.This challenges the moral of the church to become borderless and reach out, propelled by the love of Christ. This paper is an attempt to facilitate the church to become borderless by approaching the concern from the perspective of prophetic diakonia.

## 2. ROPHETIC DIAKONIA[2]

Primarily Prophets were understood as people who foretell the things to come. It is true in one way. They deciphered the signs of the times with the help of a discerning spirit and urged the people and the rulers to take decisions with justice. Their deliberations always invited the people to amend their ways and turn to God. They also spoke to the rulers not to become an ally of the oppressive rulers but believe in God and his redemption. The prophetic spirit rose in every occasion, stood against the repressive and demonic forces as an advocate of the voiceless victims. The study programme "Rethinking Ecclesia" propels the church to perform the role of the prophets.

Diakonia is a Greek word used for service. It is strongly felt that faith and works cannot be separated in Christian spirituality (Cf. James 2:17). In other words the diakonia of the church accommodate diverse works or deeds (*ergon*Cf. Matt 5:16, Ephesians 2:10). The Church of South India, understands diakonia as a mission in service with dedication. It identifies medical and educational institutions, homes for children, rural development projects and other diakonial ministries as expressions of this diakonia. Prophetic diakonia differs from patronage, alms giving and charity that do not contest the prevailing domination. Prophetic diakonia is primarily an advocacy, raising voice against the oppressive structures on behalf of the victims and secondarily furnishing egalitarian alternatives for the oppressive structures.

## 3. ADVOCACY: BECOMING THE VOICE OF THE VOICELESS

As Christian community we are well informed about the prophets of the Bible. The Almanac of the Church of South India brings to us the concerns of the Church. For instance, observation of Sunday services for girl child, child labour, bonded labour, women, dalits, poor, education ministry, healing Sunday, migration, agriculture, industrial workers, etc., These Sunday services make us aware of the plight of such people. However the congregation and the church as a structure are hesitant to take the role of Prophetic Diakonia. Let us ponder some of the constraints that prevent us from acting. Among the numerous reasons that prevail a few are taken for this study.

### *Fear*

Fear makes us to run towards safe zones and close the doors. Let us take the example of a murder committed in day light on the road. Thousands and thousands of people see it. But nobody stops the act of killing or comes forward as witness for prosecution. When Nathan came to the court of David and charged him as "you are the man" on behalf of Uriah, he was well aware of the risk he was taking (Cf. 2 Samuel 12:7). Today the death and demonic forces create fear and spread it over the community to prevent any kind of individual or organised protest against such incidents. We are led by fear not by faith. We pretend as if we are liberated by our faith but we are bound to the fear of insecurity at every moment. Fear is a major constraint that prevents us to take a prophetic role against the demonic forces.

## *Psycological Numbing*

Numbness occurs in flesh of the body. What we discuss now is the numbness that occurs in mind. Consider yourself sitting before your television for news. In Sun news channel they give the details of a rape case and you are moved, become angry and shed tears. You change the channel and hear the news from Raj news. There you get another rape case. This time your emotions decrease. You feel like changing the channel. You change the channel to Polymer news. They also present a rape case and this time there is no reaction from you. You are called for dinner and on the dinner table you say "rape is widespread because of the dressing of the girls." The flooding incidents huge in number make us insensitive and consequently inactive. We are no more sensitive. We easily pass across a hungry person, a crippled, a sick, a person bleeding. Technology made us to live in the virtual world and be insensitive to the reality.

## *Oppressor Mentality*

Society is built on relationships of various forms. There are situations when two parties participate in the life of a society with contradiction. These contradictions evolve in the production, distribution and governing relationships of a society. In the socialisation process we are exposed to such a contradiction as an oppressor and the oppressed. We inherit and use the values of the oppressor and oppressed according to our convenience and interest. Woman, who inherits the values of the oppressed when she is a daughter-in- law, inherits the values of the oppressor on becoming a mother-in-law.

The Peasant struggle in India has not gained the attention of the general public. When the food producers ask for compensation from the government the public murmurs "Did they remitted the profit gained in the past to the government? If food is not produced in India we can import cheaply from outside". The oppressor is housed in the minds of the general public. This is evident when people who are employees become employers and employ people for domestic work.

## Church and Its Prophetic Role

The church has different faces. It has gained matchless momentum in terms of its service to humanity. It is the pioneer in the fields of education, health care, orphanages and homes, higher education, technical education, etc.. The church is marvelled at as divine expressions of love and care. However, the church faces criticisms for not taking an active prophetic role. Such criticisms develop their argument by saying that the church in order to protect its property and to avail the rights and grants stipulated in the Indian constitution prefer to maintain good relationship with government officials and other local people.

At the same time one could cite contexts from the history of the church where church played the role of a prophet. Firstly, Dietrich Bonhoeffer a member and a theologian of the Confessing church of Germany under Nazi rule. Secondly, M.M.Thomas, a renounced protestant theologian, made sharp prophetic declaration on emergency in 1970. Thirdly, an open letter was written by the Moderator, Most Rev. Thomas K.Ommen to the fellow citizens on April 6, 2018, to join hands to shake the foundations of the present government working to fulfil the greed of the corporate bourgeoisie. The church has taken the prophetic role as well. Whenever the social contradiction becomes sharper and there is an emergent need to enlighten the people to take position the church has done it.

## 4. ALTERNATIVES

Alternative is a model of society that the suffering masses envisage. Alternative is a faith initiative, based on the conviction of the unseen things. In every social set up the dominant group denies the possibility of an alternative. Globalisation declares, "There is no alternative"

(TINA).But over the years the church placed alternatives before the society.

## *Early Church: Abolision of Private Property*

The church began to exist in Jerusalem soon after the day of the Pentecost, as an alternative social system in which everybody was equal and the need of everybody were taken care off. Accumulation of private property and the maintenance of private purse were strictly prohibited. The only agenda of the community was to proclaim the second coming of Jesus which was considered to be imminent.There were no divisions as Jew, Gentile, Greek, freemen, slave, men and women but all were considered as one.

## *Sophia Movement: Theocratic Rule of the State*

Pistis Sophia is a tradition based on the teachings of Jesus, Mary Magdalene and the disciples of Jesus. It is often classified under Gnostic texts. It is dated as 250-300AD. In this church tradition, the transfigured Jesus is assembled with his disciples including his mother Mary, Mary Magdalene and Martha. Sophia is a female divinity of Gnosticism. This third century theological construct had its influence in the nineteenth century. Later in history, in the communion of Russian Orthodox Church, Vladimir S. Soloviev (1853-1900) was a notable person who sought the unity of all Christians under the Orthodox Church. He made much theological articulations about Sophia. He conceived Sophia, God's wisdom to be eternal and perfect feminine.

Soloviev believed Christ might regenerate humanity and reform the world. True knowledge comes through the interconnection of empirical, rational and mystical ways. The Sophia movement held God to be the Absolute and nothing else. He exists in three personalities of Love. God is Love. As Love, he pervades the cosmos. His love is revealed in the Cosmos through logos. By the life, death and resurrection of Jesus, the connection between logos and Sophia was established, which is the relation between divine and human. Solviev declared that nations should regulate their socio political and economic relations on the basis of Christian principles.

He emphasized the theocratic rule of the state. Due to this he faced the oppression of Tsarist regime. A small group of this movement retired to desert to achieve the unity of the churches and prepare for second coming[3]. Sophia movement on the outlook though appeared philosophical; they were clear in identifying the Tsarist regime as evil and did not fail to oppose it. Even while undergoing persecution they do not give up their faith.

## *Donatists: Do not Surrender Yourself to Evil*

The Donatists named for the Berber Christian Donatus Magnus, were followers of a belief considered a schism by the catholic tradition. They lived in Roman province of Africa and flourished in the fourth and fifth centuries. The Donatists were exposed to the brutality of the Roman state after the edict of Diocletian on May 303. The edict ordered the surrender of Christian scriptures, the registration of church property and probably the destruction of church buildings (Numidia). In the autumn or in the early 304 AD the next edict came with a for the demand for emperor worship. The penalty for disobedience was death. Some congregations refused to surrender themselves to the authority and faced trials and tribulations. Some of the congregation and clergies were put into prison. During these times the congregation met and prayed for those who faced tribulations. The congregation also condemned those who surrendered to it by saying that they won't enter into the eternal bliss. This uncompromising denunciation of the worldliness and corruption of the existing state of the church and the denial of the validity of the orders and the sacraments made a crucial issue in the church.[4]

Donatists believed the Bishops who surrendered the scriptures cannot give baptism, bless the Lord's Supper or consecrate a Bishop.

Catholics believed the holiness of the sacrament lies in the holiness of God, whereas the Donatists believed it lies in the worthiness of the minister confecting it. This difference made the Christian community into Donatists and non-Donatists. In 313 the Bishop Donatus was consecrated and he gave the leadership for the movement and the movement was called after him.[5] Their approach could be termed as "No compromise with Evil" (Cf Rev. 14: 9-13).

### *Waldencians: poor in Spirit*

The origin of the name is in debate some say it has its roots in Vaux or valleys or vallis densa, shaded valley. At the same time it also conjectured to have come from Peter Waldo. Peter Waldo was a rich merchant of Lyons, who became impressed with the brevity and insecurity of life and went to a theologian to ask the way to heaven. In reply he got the words of Jesus told to the rich young man. "If you would be perfect, go, sell what you possess and give it to the poor, and you will have treasure in heaven; and come follow me" (Matt. 19:21). Waldo proceeded resolutely (1176) to carry out the command. He paid his credits, provided for his wife and children distributed the rest to the poor and started begging for his food. He made a deep study of the New Testament through a translation in his mother tongue. He started to imitate Christ. As Christ had commanded to his apostles to be in their mission during life time, taking no purse he preached in city and country side.[6]

Many were attracted by him. They called themselves "poor in Spirit" or the "Poor men of Lyons" when the Arch Bishop of Lyons forbade them to preach, Peter Aldo appealed to Pope. During Nazi regime they were actively involved in saving Jews by hiding them in mountains where the ancestor of Waldensians had their refuge. In 1975, they joined the Italian Methodist church to form the union of Waldensians and Methodist churches of the "World Alliance of Reformed Churches and of the World Methodist Council. Waldensians, by character, is a free church, which demands poverty in life style and conviction in non-compromising with evil.

### *Kibbutz: Community of Equals*

Martin Buber a Jewish Philosopher brought back this idea of community living when Israel as a country wanted to start its nation building after the World War II. In *Paths in Utopia* (1949) Buber referred to the Israeli kibbutz. Kibbutz is a cooperative agricultural community. The members of the community work in a natural environment and live together in a voluntary communion as a "bold Jewish undertaking" that proved to be "an exemplary non-failure," an example of a "utopian" socialism that works. Yet he did not ascribe ultimate success to it. His reservation stemmed from the fact that, generally, members of the kibbutz disregarded the relation between man and God, denying or doubting the existence or presence of a divine counterpart. In the interpersonal area they fulfilled God's commandment to build a just community while yet denying the divine origin of the implicit imperative. This was an attempt to ascertain the Jewish people after the holocaust.

The first kibbutz, established in 1909, was Degania. Kibbutzes were communities that were based on work rather than an ideology. The members were exclusively Jews and engaged themselves in agriculture and related activities. There was no private property among the members and they kept everything in common. The motivational ideas were the I–thou relationship between God and his people and the importance of a Jewish state. Nowadays, farming has been partly supplanted by other economic branches, including industrial plants and high-tech enterprises. Kibbutzim began as utopian communities, a combination of socialism and Zionism.[7] In recent decades, some kibbutzim have been privatized and changes have been made in the communal lifestyle. A member of a kibbutz is called a *kibbutznik*. Kibbutz was criticised for its exclusiveness to Jews. Also kibbutz does not admit gay, lesbian and children of single parent. However, one can understand the influence of Second World War and the Nazi regime in the minds of the Jews to consolidate their tradition and establish their identity. At the same time based on the faith in Yahweh, Kibbutz is a meaningful contribution for the world community to ponder.

### *Women's Dare: Solidarity Strengthens*

Globalisation controls production, marketing and consumption. It is a project of the corporate firms. The advent of big shopping malls and online marketing displaced small producers, small vendors, dalits and women from the market. The various missionary movements that came in to the country for preaching the Gospel trained many groups of women and adivasis to learn certain skills and produce for their livelihood. Women DARE (Dalit &Adivasi Rural Entrepreneurs) is introduced by CSI-SEVA to sustain these missionary initiatives alive and develop their marketing scope by bringing them to a favourable position of reaching the members of CSI. To begin with, CSI-SEVA, collected various products like handicrafts, bags, tea leaves, other curry powders, bangles, cushions, garments from every corners of CSI.

## CONCLUSION

Prophetic diakonia is basically a two folded approach. On the one hand it raises voice on behalf of the voiceless and on the other hand it furnishes new alternatives against the dominant oppressive structures. We live in a context where people are virtually connected and really separated. The advent of Globalisation increased individualism. The values nurtured by the institutions like family in the social fabric, are obliterated as those institutions themselves could not withstand against the rule of the market. This generation celebrates no values and norms.The rulers see the opposition only in the virtual world, the social media, and not in the real world. The demonic forces remain uncontested. In India till the recent past, the non-violent resistances were considered important and the administration also responded positively.

Now the administration is numb to people's cry. The rulers let loose state repression on the people asking for justice. The people in distress do not find a supporting hand. Over the years church made sincere contributions to rebuild the nation on new foundations. Will the church provide a leadership today for the people who long for a change? Will the church come to the murderous David's court to ask justice for Uriah and Bathsheba? Will the church warn the king Ahab for confiscating the land of Naboth? Is it not our priority to join hands with the head of this church, as he calls for shaking of the foundations of an unjust order? These questions remain unanswered.

## Endnotes

[1] Rethinking Ecclesia, Building Christ Communities; Towards a Borderless Church, Consultation on Prophetic Diakonia, On 15th and 16th May2018, CSI Synod Centre, Chennai.

[2] Prophetic diakonia and advocacy, https://www.cca.org.hk/prophetic-diakonia-and-advocacy/

[3] Kenneth Scott Latourette, *A History of Christianity,* (Harper and Row, Publishers, London, 1953), 1219-1220.

[4] Christopher Dawson, *Religion and the Rise of Western Culture*, (Image books, New York, 1958), 205.

[5] Bulloch J., *Pilate to Constantine,* (The Saint Andrew Press, Edinburg, 1981).325-326.

[6] Kenneth Scott LaTourette, *A History of Christianity*, (Harper& Row Publishers, London, 1953), 451.

[7] Buber, Martin, Paths in Utopia, (Syracuse University Press, New York, 1996), 142.

12

# Rethinking Ecclesia: A Liberative Homiletic Perspective

**P. Ravi**

## Introduction

What is the need for rethinking ecclesia? Are there any problems in today's ecclesia? I think the people who are calling us to think about ecclesia have concern about the problems in today's ecclesia and are attempting to travel towards a realistic ecclesia. Without analyses of the problems within the ecclesia, we cannot rethink about ecclesia.

## Etymological Studies of the Word "Ekklesia"

The Ekklessia, this Greek word is derived from the verb *ekkaleo*. It means "to summon" or to call out; the word "ek" means "out from" and "kaleo" means "to call". So ekklesia means calling out together an assembly.[1]

It is an assembly or a congregation. The ekklesia in the NT is a group of people who have been called out of the world and to God. It is an assembly or a congregation called by God to do a particular task. Now, it is called as church.

## Reason for Rethinking

In India, churches are divided along social, denominational, economic and by caste lines. The church adopted and accepted these evil systems and is practicing it. As we are calling ourselves as faith community but we are standing against the teachings of Jesus Christ in relation with faith and action that build various boundaries within ourselves.

The main boundaries we have in our church are gender bias, caste bias, economic status, and linguistic boundaries. These boundaries should be eliminated in our generation. Therefore, we have to rethink the ecclesia in today's context. In our modern world, because of globalization, internal war, ethnic issues and religious terrorism people migrate from one place to another. Migration doesn't just mean people moving about, but people are uprooted from the land they were born in, have lived, played and grown. Where ever they migrant they are not considered as human beings who belong. Sometimes the Church also views them this way.

According to Gustavo Gutierrez, if the church wishes to be faithful to the God of Jesus Christ, it must become aware of itself from below, from among the poor of this world, the exploited classes, despised ethnic groups and marginalized cultures. It must dive into the hell of this world, into communion with the misery, injustice, struggles and hopes of the wretched of the earth.[2]

Desmond Tutu said that the church is the only organization to serve the world. It has no any self-centeredness.

According to these interpretations, the ecclesia is a call for working and serving for others. It means, not only work for our people (caste, region, denomination, language) but for others. It includes not only humanbeings but nature also. That is called "holistic liberation." We could achieve this new ecclesia through educating our congregations by way of preaching.

## Homiletic

Homiletic is an art and science of preaching. It moves from text to congregations. In between text to pew, it needs some analytical interpretation and preparation for preaching.

Martin Luther defines preaching as an act of God through which God encounters God's people reminding them of God's saving act in the history[3]

For Karl Barth, preaching is word of God which he himself speaks claiming for the purpose of exposition of a biblical text in free human words that are relevant to contemporaries by those who are called to do this in the church that is obedient to his commission.[4]

For Alfred Stephen, preaching becomes word of God when it fulfills the redemptive and liberative purpose of God.[5]

As we know the boundaries which we identified in the introduction, these boundaries can be overcome through preaching.

## Functions of Liberative Homiletics

As Allen states, liberation preaching helps the congregation to understand the forces of oppression that are at work in the world as well as the interpretation of the Bible that can help analyse the world and our response to it. It helps the congregation where God is at work for liberation in today's work. It helps the congregation identify how to respond appropriately to the liberative force field. Preaching should help identify ways that help congregations to actively participate in the movement towards liberation.[6]

When we use liberative homiletic in our church, the existing boundaries can be eliminated. Liberative homiletics can educate the people of ecclesia to eradicate the oppressed factors within the churches to build a borderless church.

## Theoretical Issues in Liberative Homiletics

To come out from the boundaries to borderless church, the following theoretical issues would be helpful.

## Hermeneutics of Metanoia[7]

The Reign of God is a call to live the will of God. God's will is to love all the people. If we do not love created beings, we are against the law of God. Lovelessness, hatred, enemity are the great problems within the church. It is also called sin against not only human beings but against God. These should be eradicated from the church. Without denying the reality of individual sin, the liberation preacher concentrates on the structural aspects of sin, which is the macro-structures that bring about social injustice, poverty and violence around the world.[8]

To addresss structural sin each and every member of the church requires Metanoia in their heart. These issues should be explored in our liberative preaching. For example, after John the Baptist was arrested, Jesus in his first preaching said, "the time is fulfilled and the kingdom of God is at hand; ***repent and believe in the gospel***. Without changing the personal and the societal transformation, there is no borderless church. So, the hermeneutics of Metanoia is very needed in our today's context.

## Hermeneutics of Hope

Hope is nothing but the vision of the future even though living in the present that seems bad. The ecclesia is called to ensure the betterment of the afflicted communities. According to Moltmann, hope is the understanding of the ground reality and requires the faith oriented action for transforming the world to break down the boundaries.[9]

The hermeneutics of hope needs to call the congregation to know the reality and then to stimulate them to think and raise their voice against the reality. This leads to struggle against injustice to attain the hope. The liberative preaching can be a tool to bring the hope of the marginalized people of the ecclesia. The scripture text should be interpreted and taught according to the hermeneutics of hope.

## Hermeneutics of Sacrifice

In our church, each and every congregation is running to obtain the benefits from the church. But, sacrifice does not seek benefit. Sacrifice is giving ourselves to the benefit of others. Jesus also came for redemption and liberation for creation. He gives his life without selfishness for the betterment of the world. And, the disciples of Jesus also gave their life to establish the Reign of God, not for themselves. Here, the meaning of the ecclesia is called out from the evil society by God to work for the transformation of the world. For this work, every member of the faith community needs to sacrifice themselves for making the Reign of God a reality. In our preaching, this should be considered as a main concern. The liberation preaching should motivate the people to a sacrificial life.

## Conclusion

God is not a God for a particular people. God created human beings in his image and he gave his breath to them. So, the people who are living in the cosmos all are created by God. So all are our brothers and sisters. Jesus the Christ does not belong to Christian community only. He is the Christ for the whole world. He gave himself for the redemption of the people. The Holy Spirit is the spirit that is at work when we work for others and when we sacrifice ourselves for the betterment of the world the spirit comes with us. Hence, God, Christ, Holy Spirit and the church do not belong to particular groups. We cannot make boundary around this God, Christ and Holy Spirit. If there are no boundaries between them then we too should not make boundaries between ourselves in the name of caste, colour and creed. A true ecclesia believes that boundaries and borders are sin; Repents and believes in the borderless church and works to make it a reality.

## Endnotes

[1] Joseph A. Komonchak, Mary Collins, Dermot A. Lane (eds) *The New Dictionary of Theology* (Bangalore: Theological Publication in India, 2006), 186.

[2] Gustavo Gutierrez, *The Power of the Poor in History* (London: SCM press, 1983), 211.

[3] Alfred Stephen, *Homiletics: Handbook for Teachers and Learners of Preaching* (Nagaland: TTCC and ECHO-Forest, 2017),12.

[4] Alfred Stephen, *Homiletics: Handbook for Teachers,*12.

[5] Alfred Stephen, *Homiletics: Handbook for Teachers,* 13.

[6] Ronald J.Allen, *Thinking Theologically* (Minneapolis: Fortress Press, 2008), 76.

[7] The word Metanoia means the change of heart, repent.

[8] Marcella Althaus-Reid, *The Oxford Companion to Christian Thought* (NY: Oxford University Press, 2000), 388.

[9] Jurgen Moltmann, *The Theology of Hope* (London: SCM Press,1969), 35-36.

## Bibliography

Allen, Ronald J. *Thinking Theologically*. Minneapolis: Fortress Press, 2008.

Althaus-Reid, Marcella. *The Oxford Companion to Christian Thought.* NY:Oxford University Press, 2000

Gutierrez, Gustavo. *The Power of the Poor in History.* London: SCM Press, 1983.

Komonchak, Joseph A., Mary Collins, Dermot A. Lane., eds. *The New Dictionary of Theology.* Bangalore: Theological Publication in India, 2006.

Moltmann, Jurgen. *The Theology of Hope.* London: SCM Press,1969.

Stephen, Alfred. *Homiletics: Handbook for Teachers and Learners of Preaching.* Nagaland: TTCC and ECHO-Forest, 2017.

13

# Missiology for Borderless Church

**R. Christopher Rajkumar**

"Borderless Church" is a church that holds a missionary character in today's globalized and post-modern contexts. This observation of David Lundy (2005) points out that the primary focus of the borderless church is that it exists for others by encouraging and equipping one to live by "gospel values" in society as people (not as institution). The "bottom line" for the borderless church is nothing but "Moving 'from' ... 'to' i.e. moving from both the mission / Church, Seminary, mission compounds and such, to the Society. With this agenda missiologists and theologians are called to articulate theologies of "appropriating God relevantly" to free the weak and the oppressed through theological conversations publicly and sensually in communities at large rather than limiting these to seminaries, classrooms and mission compounds. With such a view the "Basel Mission" traditions and practices, as compared the popular / traditional mission compound mission(s), facilitated a paradigm shift by setting their missional and theological priorities of moving towards a "borderless" mission.

David Lundy describes five (missionary) characters of the borderless church.

- Church exists primarily for those outside it, both locally and worldwide;
- Encourages a vibrant religious / spiritual life as honouring God;
- It is more of larger community rather than small congregations / groups;
- Emphsis on preaching and practicing the "Word";
- Equipping the people of God (laity) for mission and ministry.

Conversations on borderless world globally were initiated by Kenichi Ohmae (economist) According to him "borderless" is more of a "glocal" concept where the economy transcends time and space simultaneously globally and locally. If we try to translate this concept from the Christian missional perspective, the 'message and the value of the gospel of Christ relates to communities and people both globally, locally and demographically.

## Migration and Mission

From a missional perspective, today's human "migrations" (Middle east, Africa, Latin America, South Asia and others) shape the mission agenda for the churches and will continue to chart the course of mission in coming years. The borderless church concept gives new perspectives on human societies, bypassing the timeworn categories and frameworks of traditional and popular missions. This process also known as "connectography," connects "us" as borderless beings; as living and existing with the flow of people with their faiths and traditions constituting our constantly evolving reality. So connectography helps us to understand time, space and people around and beyond us in the midst of rapid mobility and technological inter-dependency.

## Cyber Mission: Borderless in Nature

Cyber mission is one such mission of connectography which is borderless in nature. The National Council of Churches in India (NCCI) jointly with the World Association of Christian Communication (WACC) initiated a missional conversation on "Cyber Mission" among the Indian mission movements. Rev. Dr. Peter Singh presented a paper on Cyber Mission titled "Social Media: An emerging new Location for Christian mission to the Digital Natives". In his paper Dr. Peter Singh, mentioned those who live in cyber space and called them the "cyber natives" or the "digital natives" who already live in a borderless concept. He opined that practicing the Christian mission in this context of several social networking possibilities where people are not merely consumers but also active creators of information can be very challenging. On the other hand, the 4th Industrial revolution is using the virtual "space", "robotization" and "humanoids" to serve society with artificial intelligence from remote controls and remote monitoring. However, cyber missiologists suggest, in obedience to Jesus' call to the church to proclaim the gospel to all nations (borders) and people (Matt 28:16–20) the churches and mission organizations must rise to claim the opportunities and challenges that social media provides, taking due consideration of the strengths and weaknesses of cyber (virtual) space which has no borders, and develope new strategies and methodologies that will serve the church well in the 21st century.

## Traditional, Popular and Modern Mission Focus

Traditionally, the focus of mission is polarized or dichotomized thereby resulting in a separation between concepts:

- "saving the soul" or the "social gospel";
- "church planting" or "Christian charity / diaconia";
- "paternalism" or "indigenization";

- "long-term missions" or "short-term missions";
- "career-missionaries" or "tent-makers."

Conceptually, traditional mission paradigm is "territorial," meaning that there is a sharp distinction between "here" and "there." It has a "lineal" meaning, where a movement goes one way from "sending" to "receiving," or from "assimilation" to "amalgamation." Moreover, the perspective of the traditional mission paradigm is geographically divided into foreign mission versus home mission, urban versus rural, or state/nation versus country/state. As a discipline, there is a compartmentalization between "theology of missions" and "strategy of missions." The priority of traditional mission is to reach "unreached people groups" in the most "unreached" regions of the world. Whereas the cyber missiology considers all equal.

## Borderless Missiology

The globalization theory has moved beyond the limited confines of the political geography discourse, crossing its own disciplinary boundaries. Until now it has not beensuccessful in creating a common language or glossary of terms and promoting "mono culture". However, borderless missiology affirms diversity and plurality. Borderless missiology recognizes that, in our world shaped by multiculturalism and pluralism it is important that Christ's witnesses become interculturally competent and develop relational skills to bridge and build authentic relationships to be the theology of borderless mission and borderless church.

The proposed new paradigm of "borderless missiology" is not to replace "traditional missiology", but to supplement it in response to the new demographic reality of the 21st century. It is not a case of "either / or" mutually exclusive options; but a "both /and" inclusive combination. For further discussion on "both / and" framework emerging from the "Trinitarian paradigm" there is also a new "relational paradigm' that goes with "borderless missiology.

Actually, the history of Indian missions affirms borderless missiology as the Most Rev. Dr. P C Singh observes: The Indian mission history witnesses and affirms that, the Indian mission has a borderless nature and is not to the margins (borders), rather it is, mission 'Of' the margins, mission 'By' the margins and mission 'With' the margins.

When mission is geared to work towards the borderless church, it is not only lineal (here "To" there) but polycentric where we affirm church "Of" all and church "for" all, that accepts others as they are and practices hospitality by becoming and being a welcoming church /mission. Borderless missiology considers the "outside" people / communities as agents of transformation and (equal) partners in mission, not as target groups. It refers to the open society where the communities bring renaissance, influence and change upon people and the society.

In the midst of our learning process, borderless missiology could be a framework for understanding and participating in God's liberative mission among the people living outside of our (mission) compounds. It suggests a paradigm shift from the "Great Commission" to the "Great Commandment".

## Borderless Mission: Icon of Inclusion

According to contemporary study of borders, there are notions such as "borders are institutions". Border terminologies focus on the binary distinction between "us" and "them", the "included" and "excluded". This should be studied not only from a top-down perspective but also from the bottom-up perspective with a focus on the individual border narratives and experiences, reflecting the ways in which borders impact the daily life and practices of people living in and around the borderland and trans - boundary transition zones.

Rt. Rev. Dr. Daniel Thiyagaraja, Bishop of CSI Jaffna Diocese yearns for a borderless church and as the "mission of a borderless church," adds anything of substance to what the church today needs to become more truly church by extending and establishing relationships for transformation of self and others into the inclusive and borderless and to embrace Christ's new creation.

The borderless church is - Church "Of" all, Church "for" all which includes all (the socially, religiously, historically, traditionally, politically, economically and culturally excluded communities). Some such concrete examples are CSI's Disability Intervention in Solidarity and Holistic Accompaniment (DISHA) initiative of the diaconal wing of CSI which is called SEVA and SEVA's other interventions like the CSI Girl Child Campaign and CSI Child rights campaign and initiatives of other organizations for Children At Risk, NCCI's Indian Disability Ecumenical Accompaniment (IDEA) initiative and the National Ecumenical Forum of Gender and Sexual Diversities (NEFGSD) of the NCCI and the World Council of Churches' Ecumenical Diaconia' and such.

## Conclusion

The envisioned "borderless Church", despite exciting possibilities and potential could also be rendered insubstantial or even irrelevant unless there is a radical paradigm shift to participate, promote and practice inclusion. So the CSI's process of initiating this theological, missiological and diaconal discussion on "Borderless Churches" will pave way for such expected paradigm shifts.

## Bibliography

Lundy, David. Borderless Church: Shaping the Church in the 21st Century. Waynesboro, Ga: Authentic Media, 2005.

<www.csijaffnadiocese.org/downloads/bible-study-borderless.doc> (15 Feb 2018)

<https://csisynod.com/news_view.php?id=5561> (15 Feb 2018)

<http://ncci1914.com/2017/03/29/indian-mission-movements-called-minister-among-cyber-natives/> (15 Feb 2018)

<https://www.oikoumene.org/en/press-centre/news/ecumenical-diaconia-sharing-gods-gifts-at-all-tables> (15 Feb 2018)

14

# Diaspora Missiology for a Borderless Church

**K. S. Shaiju Kumar**

The term "diaspora" is etymologically derived from the Greek word *diaspora* or *diaspeirein* (dispersion) and has historically been used to refer to the scattering and dispersion of Jews in the OT and Christians in the NT. In contemporary literature the word is used to describe the phenomenon of people on the move or being moved. Diaspora is a global phenomenon yet diaspora missiology begins at a local level and proceeds to the global in perspective. Diaspora missiology is "the systematic and academic study of the phenomenon of diaspora in the fulfillment of God's mission." The term and concept of "diaspora missiology" is descriptive of people's residence being different from that of their "place of origin" without prejudice or confusion.

## Biblical Understanding About Diaspora

Migration is one of the important themes in the Bible that reflects the stories of the migration of individuals, families and nations. God travels with the diaspora communities (Gen 46:4) and He used foreigners and immigrants – Joseph, Daniela, Esther, Paul, and others."[1] God uses migration of his people as a method of mission to make them a blessing among other communities.

In OT the stories of diaspora include Adam and Eve (Gen 3:21–23); Cain after murdering Abel (Gen 4:14–17); God's command to Noah and family to fill the earth (Gen 9:1); construction of the Tower of Babel, the divine punishment and dispersion of the people (Gen 11:7-9); diaspora of the families of Abraham and other Patriarchs; story of Joseph: a model of forceful migration; people of Israel living in exile in different periods. According to OT Law, even though there were provisions for supporting aliens, they were listed along with poor and widows and counted among the most marginalized.

NT stories of diaspora include Jesus who became a refugee immediately after his birth (Matt 2:13); the holy family is the model for all diaspora communities; Jesus sending his disciples to all nations; dispersed Christian communities (persecuted) gathering in their new contexts and starting small groups to worship God. Through diaspora, Christian faith was spread to all nations.

## Diaspora Missiology

"Diaspora Missiology" is "a missiological framework for understanding and participating in God's redemptive mission among people living outside their place of origin."[2] Diaspora Missiology necessitates interdisciplinary study of academic fields related to who, what, when, where, and how populations are moving (e.g. anthropology, demography, economics, geography, history, law, political science, and sociology) and classic missiological study (e.g. theology, missiology, biblical studies, evangelism). Enoch Wan in his book *Diaspora Missiology: Theory, Methodology, and Practice* identifies three types of diaspora missions:

1. Missions to the diaspora: reaching the diaspora groups themselves;

2. Missions through the diaspora: diaspora Christians reaching out to their kinsmen wherever they are;

3. Missions by and beyond the diaspora: motivating and mobilizing diaspora Christians for cross-cultural missions.[3]

"My ancestor was a wandering Aramean" (Deut 26:5) is the foundational faith expression of the Israelite community. Diaspora missiology affirms that God was with his people while they were diaspora and God is the liberator of all marginalized groups. Jesus was an immigrant and showed that all his disciples should accept and love immigrants. For instance he said, "I was a stranger and you welcomed me" (Matt 25:35). Diaspora missiology affirm that all people are created in the image of God, especially immigrants of both genders. Diaspora missiology is rooted on theological anthropology and it always maintains a social commitment to all people. This theology always interrogates all inequalities in a society that dehumanizes people in the name of caste, colour, language and ethnicity. Christians must embrace a "Kingdom orientation" missiology as opposed to a parochial approach. In diaspora missions, divisions are minimized between the host and the diaspora. The trademark of "diaspora missions" in action is to combine the second part of the Great Commandment of "love your neighbour" as powerful in pre-evangelistic efforts to carrying out the Great Commission of making disciples of all nations.

## Attitude of Church Towards Diaspora

The church often perceives immigrants as illiterate, uncivilized, unskilled and as root causes of disturbances in our society such as theft, sexual abuse, killing etc. When we visit their homes, they treat us like kings and noble people. However, we ask them to stay outside our gates and ask them what they want. We consider them untrustworthy and we are reluctant to help them. We entertain unfounded fears that if we help them they will become dependent on us for all their needs.

Church has sometimes been reluctant to help immigrants because we fear retribution from other religious fundamentalists.

## Immigrants and Their Problems

There are many patterns of diaspora, such as people displaced because of war and famine, urbanization, migration, immigration, etc. People move on voluntary basis for education, freedom, economic advancement, etc. People are also being moved on an involuntary basis when they are forced to move as in the case of refugees and victims of human trafficking. They move because of personal and/or non-personal reasons.[4]

Migrants and refugees endure many hardships and most would prefer to return home under more favourable circumstances. They are ready to take any risk and sacrifice to support their families by earning money while being diaspora. They work more hours than they would normally work if they were in their home countries. Yet most of them are cheated by their contractors or bosses.

Minho Song says, "Finding themselves aliens in a new setting, diaspora Christians have the natural tendency to stay amongst themselves because they find comfort and a sense of belonging to their kind. This homogeneous pull brings and binds them together, but ultimately bans then from meaningfully participating in the lives of those who are outside of the group."[5] Unfamiliarity with the local culture is another barrier. The newcomers lack the social cues to know when and how it is appropriate to enter into a conversation about spiritual things. Another major reason for alienation from loal culture and people is unfamiliarity with the local language. Most people hesitate to express themselves when they know that they cannot speak a language well. Often the cultural gap between the local people and the diaspora people results in prejudice of one towards the other.

## Christ Communities and Their Mission Among the Immigrants

The tasks of missiologists and missions leaders is to realize the scale, frequency and intensity of people moving both internally and internationally. Missiologists need to integrate factual findings with missiological understanding in ministry planning and missions strategy.

There are some options churches have for engaging with immigrant believers. Those are: integrating immigrants fully into existing churches, sharing facilities with immigrant congregation members, assisting immigrant believers to form their own Independent Churches, and lastly developing multicultural churches which can integrate people from many cultures.

The most important first step is to accept immigrants as one among us and accept our present multi-linguistic, multi-religious and multi-cultural context as a new ministry context. Respect the language, religion and culture of the immigrants. Prepare multi-cultural congregations to provide them spiritual strength. Practice hospitality; provide food of different taste to create a homely atmosphere in our church campuses and events. Provide the service of missionaries or church leaders who have the ability to translate the word of God based on the framework of diaspora theology/missiology.

Diaspora gatherings should be an ecumenical one and must respect people of other religious traditions. We could provide support for their initial stay, health care and legal immigration issues and offer support through counseling, prayer and awareness programmes. All missionaries or pastors should learn the legal safety legislations to help support neighbours from different states in India. A Christ community should take the risk to provide space and support to the immigrants. We must include prayers on behalf of migrants and refugees in the general intercessions each week. The CSI could develop a "Parish Welcoming Plan" that could help welcome the newly arrived parishioners with host welcoming events, visits to newcomers to the parish community, and organizing outreach activities directed towards migrant populations in the community. A congregation could plan multicultural liturgies, sacramental services, and intercessions, outreach and training for members of all ethnic groups as parish ministers and provide multilingual resources and materials to address the pastoral needs of migrant populations. We could organize charitable drives to benefit migrants and refugees. Churches could also plan a parish service day in migrant and refugee neighbourhoods.

## Missiological Implications of Diaspora Communities

Diaspora people are people in transition - migrants and immigrants taken away from the comfort and security of their homeland. They are more receptive to change including conversion to another faith that is welcoming. Some are in dire need, especially the displaced people and victims of human trafficking. Carrying out the Great Commandment by offering hospitality and caring for their psycho-social and economic needs will be highly effective to showcase our faith as a welcoming community with these people groups. Churches in "receiving countries/ states" therefore are presented with an opportunity to practice "mission at our doorstep" to reach them, without crossing borders geographically, linguistically and culturally. This is the "ministering to the diaspora" aspect of practicing "diaspora missions."

Furthermore,"ministering through and beyond the diaspora" are two additional aspects of practicing "diaspora missions." These two approaches are to be employed in order to seize the new opportunities created by the phenomenon of diaspora. Dispersed Christian communities could be mobilized to carry out the Great Commission through proper education and training. As diaspora groups become proficient in the language and culture of their host society, they can serve as the natural bridges for "ministry beyond them" to reach other people in their host societies and countries. Ministering to receptive people among the diaspora strategically (i.e.

ministering to the diaspora) and mobilizing diasporic congregations for missions (i.e. minister through the diaspora) are aspects of good Christian stewardship.

## Conclusion

Ministering to migrants offers new frontiers to announce the gospel and to witness to our Christian faith, while showing profound respect for other faith traditions. These encounters are fertile ground for developing sincere ecumenical and inter-religious relations.

Churches find ourselves sadly ineffective in impacting people from other cultures. Often local believers and our churches do little to connect with or encourage diaspora believers. This is largely due to cultural and linguistic differences, but most often people in the host culture simply don't "see" the diaspora community.

The Church must be a vigilant advocate, defending against any unjust restriction of the natural right of individual persons to move freely within their own nation and from one nation to another. Attention must be called to the rights of immigrants and their families and respect for their human dignity. Migrants should be met with a hospitable and welcoming attitude which can encourage them to become part of the Church's life, always with due regard for their freedom and their specific cultural identity.

## Endnotes

[1] Ed Slivoso, "Testimonial" in *Blessed Migrants* by Samuel Lee (Bloomington, IN: iUniverse, 2008), ix

[2] "The Seoul Declaration on Diaspora Missiology" <http://www.lausanne.org/documents/seoul-declaration-on-diaspora-missiology.html> (15 Feb 2018)

[3] Enoch Wan, "Introduction," in *Diaspora Missiology: Theory, Methodology, and Practice* (ed. Enoch Wan; Portland,OR: Institute of Diaspora Studies, 2011), 5.

[4] David Lundy, *Borderless Church: Shaping the Church for the 21st Century.* (UK: Authentic. 2005) xiv.

[5] Minho Song, "The Diaspora Experience of the Korean Church and its Implications for World Missions," in *Korean Diaspora and Christian Mission* (eds. S. Hun Kim and Wonsuk Ma; Eugene, OR: Wipf and Stock Publishers, 2011), 125.

## Bibliography


Lee, Samuel. *Blessed Migrants.* Bloomington, IN: iUniverse, 2008.

Lundy, David. *Borderless Church: Shaping the Church for the 21st Century.* UK: Authentic. 2005.

Song, Minho. "The Diaspora Experience of the Korean Church and its Implications for World Missions." Page 125 in *Korean Diaspora and Christian Mission.* Edited by S. Hun Kim and Wonsuk Ma. Eugene, OR: Wipf and Stock Publishers, 2011.

Wan, Enoch. *Diaspora Missiology: Theory, Methodology, and Practice.* Portland, OR: Institute of Diaspora Studies, 2011.

"The Seoul Declaration on Diaspora Missiology" <http://www.lausanne.org/documents/seoul declaration-on-diaspora-missiology.html> (15 Feb 2018)

15

# Rethinking Ecclesia: From Border to Broader Church

**Vinod Allen**

Stanly J. Samartha while writing the Foreword to *From Jerusalem to New Delhi*, says:

> The history of the Christian Church is a subject of interest and inspiration to all Christians. It is the story of a small group of people going out into lands far and near inviting others to join the fellowship of their faith in Jesus Christ. It is an account of the Church's attempts to express the fundamentals of its faith in different cultural contexts. It is also a constant reminder of the Church's need for reformation, at all times in the light of God's Word.[1]

Samrtha is right in saying that the Church needs reformation at all times and it has to be in the light of the word of God. By the concept "Rethinking *Ecclessia*" we are saying we need a reformation. Ratnakara Sadananda says, "At times we share borders, we cross borders, we merge borders, we re-draw borders, we dream of border-less-ness…"[2] At the same time he agrees, "Borders do exist". So there is a need for rethinking *Ecclessia* to re-draw the borders towards borderless Church.

There are many a definitions for the Church – *Ecclesia*. Basically, it is a called out community. In the ancient Greek world this was a significant and powerful body of the common people, which had "Liberty and Equality" as its goal. We can also define it as a faith/faith confessing community, a witnessing community, a healing community, a sharing community and many more according to the contexts of the people. Ecclesia was often indicated or identified with the clerical order which eventually led to an understanding of the history of the Church as the history of the ecclesiastical institution. As years went by, this thinking progressed to an understanding of the Church as a people. Consequently, the history of the Church is the history of a people's corporate response to the challenges of the gospel and their living as a growing community in constant dialogue with the religions and cultures in which they live.[3]

Here one has to rethink our past from an ecumenical perspective taking seriously the process of unity. This means historians should take up seriously the challenge to bring the past alive and bring it to bear on ecumenical issues that we face today. History is a bridge between the past and the present, therefore, this paper is a modest attempt to find a means to achieve borderless *Ecclesia* in the days to come.

From the first century A.D. the Church began its growth. In Matt 28:20 we read Jesus' Great Commission that says "To make disciples". He did not mention any borders there. Luke in Acts 1:8 explains how the disciples were further strengthened by the Holy Spirit to become witnesses to the whole universe without any borders. However soon borders arose one after another starting with the issue of serving Greek widows in the Church, the issue of circumcision, authority and order in local Churches, divisions in the form of party politics (Paul's group and Appolo's group) and so on. In 313 A.D. the "Edict of Milan" ushered in yet another phase to Christianity which eventually led the Church to many heresies, disputes and divisions. Subsequently, there were five Church Councils during the 4th and 5th centuries to settle these issues. Later in 1054 A.D. the Church was clearly divided into the Western Church and the Eastern Church.

The Western Church was further divided into Catholic Church and Protestant Church in 1529 A.D. There came radical Protestantanism, during 16th and 17th centuries, which paved way to great revival movements called Pietism (Europe), Evangelical Awakening (Britain) and Great Awakening (America). These great movements were also called the Evangelical Awakening, which resulted in the Missionary Movement during the 18th century. Ruth Rouse and Stephen Neil say, "The Evangelical awakening knew no boundaries. It crossed Atlantic Ocean; it spread from country to country."[4] It is recorded that there were more than 150 missionary organizations working in India during the period 1834-1900. Many missionary societies invented themselves as the agents of new civilizations. They also asserted their identity as the labourers in the kingdom of God and so on. When the Western Christian missionaries arrived India they made their own borders. The Indians were perceived as "heathens" living in darkness and they (the missionaries) brought the light of the gospel. "Heathen" in the view of missionaries signified religious and moral and a cultural degradation of people. Further, they divided India into geographical territories and started their work. Later on they also brought out the "Comity Arrangement" to solidify such artificially created borders. Many denominations were started by each missionary society. The missionaries even decided that one missionary organization would work in a particular vicinity where no other missionaries work. Their converts were put in their own "mission compound," in other words, "the Christian Village Community". This became yet another border because it had a different ethos altogether from the local culture of the converts. This was the picture of the *Ecclessia* in the middle of the 19th century India where denominationalism was much probably much more prevalent here than in other countries.

The Indian attempts for unity of the Church in India were tremendous. Kalichran Banerjee, Dr Pulney Andy, Vedanayakam Samuel Azariah, Pandipeddi Chenchiah and Kanakarayan Tiruselvam Paul were the pioneer leaders of the rethinking movement in Indian

Christianity. This movement led the rethinking process in the context of developing Indian expressions of Biblical faith and a life as against the Western mind of denominationalism. As a result there came into existence, the Bengal Christian Association for the Promotion of Christian Trust and Godliness, Calcutta (1876), the National Church of Madras (1886) and the Christo Samaj of Calcutta (1887). These were vivid expressions of their resentment to the western missionary imperialism and denominationalism. Kaj Baggo recognizes that "It was this protest, which made the missionary societies realize the necessity of cooperation and of Church unity"[5] Generally the credit of discussions which led to the ecumenical movement have been given to western missionaries in the end of the 19th century. But the real root lies in the Indian rethinking processes which was a significant landmark in the entire Christendom.

The twentieth century was called an Ecumenical Century. It witnessed several ecumenical endevours. This began in 1901 by the Presbyterian Federation in South India called South India United Church (S.I.U.C.) Then a similar one among the Congregationalists in 1904. This followed a greater union on 24 July 1908 which was called the S.I.U.C.. The formation of the United Theological College, Bangalore can also be reckoned as an important point in the ecumenical journey. The 1910 World Missionary Conference (WMC) at Edinburgh stands as one of the great stepping stones in the history of ecumenism. The slogan that WMC raised, "Doctrine divides, service unites," paved the way to a scenario leaning towards ecumenical thinking and practices. Formation of International Missionary Council, Life and Work, Faith and Order, the Kerala United Theological Seminary, the CSI ( S.I.U.C. and C.I.P.B.C.), World Council of Churches (WCC), East Asia Christian Conference (EACC) - later known as - Christian Conference of Asia (CCA), the Second Vatican Council of the Catholic Church, the CNI and the Communion of Churches in India are certain visible manifestations of ecumenical thinking and practices of the last century.

The 21st century is looking forward to further ecumenical paradigms and praxis. The CSI is initiating this herculean task. It is high time to rethink *Ecclesia*. The Church has to have reformation, whenever needed and it has to be in the light of the word of God. Then what is its extent to which reformation could go? The ecumenical mantras are changing from time to time. For example, "Doctrine divides Ministry Unites", "Dioctrine divides, love Unites", "Doctrine divides concern for Justice Unites", "Doctrine divides, ecological concern Unites" and so on. The meaning of *Oikumene* – referring to all inhabited Universe gives a clear direction towards Borderlessness.

Above all the question to remains, "How is it possible to become a Borderless Church and to what extent?" I would like to raise certain questions here that would be pertinent in our journey towards borderless church:

1. Borders do exist. We need to re-draw the borders towards a borderless Church. What would be our principles?
2. The formation of the CSI took 28 long years, despite four basic principles (Lambeth Quadrilateral) before the leaders. What would be our Basic Principles towards a Borderless Church? They have to emerge out of our discussions and deliberations.
3. The CSI was formed mainly to witness Christ in India. Let us look at ourselves and try to analyse how we practice borderlessness in our own witnessing life? Can we give up the practice of caste system in the CSI? Can we avoid nepotism, corruption and political alignments for power within the CSI?

S. Manickam while concluding his writing on the history of the CSI stated, "Unless setting our own house in order, the Church of South India cannot aspire to be a true leaven of unity in the life of India."[6]

## Endnotes

[1] Stanly J. Samartha, "Foreward" in M.E.Gibbs, *From Jerusalem to New Delhi* (Madras: CLS,1964),v.

[2] D. Ratnakara Sadandanda, Introduction to "Towards a Borderless Church…" (Concept Paper) no date.)

[3] T. V. Philip, "Christianity in India since 1858" in *Christianity in India – a History in Ecumenical Perspective* (ed.H.C. Perumalil and E.R. Hambye (India: Prakasam Publications, 1973), 300

[4] Ruth Rouse & Stephen Neil, *The History of Ecumenical Movement 1517-1948* (London: SPCK, 1967), 310.

[5] Kaj Baggo, "The First Independence Movement Among Christians"*ICHR I/I* (June, 1967):66.

[6] S. Manickam, "Formation of the Church of South India: Historical Foundations", in *United to Unite (*CSI Synod: 1997) 25.

## Bibliography

Baggo, Kaj. "The First Independence Movement Among Christians" *ICHR I/I* (June, 1967):66.

Gibbs, M. E. *From Jerusalem to New Delhi.* Madras: CLS,1964.

Manickam, S. "Formation of the Church of South India: Historical Foundations", in *United to Unite (*CSI Synod: 1997) 25.

Philip, T. V. "Christianity in India since 1858" Page 300 in *Christianity in India – a History in Ecumenical Perspective.* Edited by H.C. Perumalil and E.R. Hambye. India: Prakasam Publications, 1973.

Rouse, Ruth & Stephen Neil. *The History of Ecumenical Movement 1517-1948*. London: SPCK, 1967.

Sadandanda, D. Ratnakara. Introduction to "Towards a Borderless Church…" no date.

16

# Youth Rethinking Ecclesia: Seeking Truth and Doing Justice

**Solomon Paul. J**

We constantly hear of controversies concerning the political, cultural, and economic borders in this world. Borders are central features in current international disputes relating to security, migration, trade, and natural resources. As communities evolve borders are defined and redefined as a way of life. Borders - physical, social or cultural - provide a safe space to a particular community while it also excludes the "other." The growing walls of division and exclusive attitudes that shun people considered as the "other" seems to be the norm of the day as the world faces huge refugee crises and displacement due to war and violence.

Today's young people are expected to grow up in such a context of distrust and misinformation. The alarming aspect of such a context of borders is that borders based on distrust controls profit, occupies and exploits people, planet, minds, bodies. They can be political, economic, financial, military, cultural and religious but the comonality is that such borders bring death and destruction to many and wealth and security to a few.

These cultures have captured the attitudes, actions and allegiances of young people making them only "consumers" and not "citizens". The recent events of hate and violence in India are normalizing this culture and the order of the day. In this kind of a context the call for young people is to "seek truth and do Justice". It is a call to search and re-search for facts, for stories from the perspective of the victims, for careful study and taking a courageous stand that the Church can only take through its young people.

Being young is an integral part of each human being. It is an integral part of one's identity. Ontologically it belongs to our humanity. When people are young at heart, they will keep their youth, even though their youthful years pass and they become adults or older people. Similarly one who feels old will behave and act as an older person. Therefore being potentially adult and old is embedded in every child and each young person, just as our childhood and youth stays within us for the whole of our life. Having said that though, it would not be amiss to say one's youth is still the "*kairos*" - a very opportune time for action and reflection, distinct from other stages of one's life. Youth is a distinctive phase due to its characteristics e.g. longing for love and acceptance, searching for meaning, openness, excitement, activity, creativity, hope, pursuing development, expecting the future that is to come, etc.) but yet, these are inseparable from the totality of being human[1].

Unfortunately churches, theologians, as well as those involved in youth ministry, see young people more or less only from the perspective of formation and development and from the perspective of what they shall become, instead of who they already are[2]. Young people today are crossing borders of culture, caste and creed in terms of affirming humanness in the other. They are already actively involved in the present in the ways they are relating and building communities around them.

## Youth As Agents not Just Recipients of Theology

The most important shift towards a theological vision of youth in Christianity emerges when young people are recognized not merely as receivers of theology designed by ecclesial (theological as well as ministerial) concerns of adults, but rather as its active agents. Young people could produce their specific theology, and it can be relevant for the whole believing community, even for professional theologians or religious educators. It is not by seeking what theologians think young people should be from a theological perspective, but one must constantly attempt to hear their authentic voices. The church must seek to understand who young people actually are, and who they want to be.

Youth theology represents a new mode of contextual theology emphasizing the abilities of young people to theologise and get involved in the complex theological process of interpreting faith, scripture and tradition within particular denominations and contextual realities. Theology was always perceived as an intellectual and reflexive way of dealing with the reality of Christian faith. It should therefore not be reserved only for the theological elite or theologically trained persons but open to all believers (including youth) to be theologians and have a right to theologise.

In this sense youth theology is an expression of active participation in the process of theologising. It should be young people themselves, who search for, and create their own theological language and expressions, communicating scripture, sharing theological insights, and understanding the faith from their own perspective. Young people are not theologically impotent, and thus, any attempt to bring them a theology as something they do not have starts with the wrong assumption. They are able to think critically and reflectively about theological questions, but maybe not in the way adults (and even they) would expect. Young people may do theology without considering that it is theology, and it is the task of professional theology to open up for young people their unsuspected abilities and help them to see themselves as theologians.

Today the church and its theological education should adopt a three dimensional approach of recognizing and doing theology of young people, theology with young people and theology for young people.[3]

## Rethinking Praxis Oriented Theology for the Youth

Encountering young people and their modus of life and their "culture" challenges traditional theological disciplines, including fundamental and practical theology, to employ a new language, new styles, and explore new ways of communicating their contents. If adults and professionals are able to listen to young people, they will be also able to see them as they really are. This will create space for mutual sharing and dialogue. It will enable all those who want to participate, to talk and exchange convictions, experiences, visions and expectations. For that purpose, traditional or professional theology can facilitate youth ministry, which has a magnificent experience of encountering young people. Exchange of theories and practices between theologians and youth could be very important for both. Only through such multidimensional engagement, mutual learning and exchange of experiences may traditional theology enable creation of a theology that could be really for youth. Youth in theological perspective are young people who narrate theological stories of their lives, and who live their Christianity in an authentic way.

## Re-developing God Consciousness Among Young People

*For in him we live and move and exist, as even some of your own poets have said, 'For we also are his children.* (Acts 17:28).

Young people of the church need to be nurtured in God consciousness. The very understanding of God is about consciousness. The aspect of growing with this consciousness enables young people to locate their existence and purpose of their living on this earth. It is through the God consciousness young people are also able to relate to each other within the community of believers.

This makes it imperative that the church needs to be aware of what type of God consciousness we have imbibed and nurture among young people. Questions like who is God? How does God function? And what kind of perceptions one holds about God? - are questions which cannot be neglected. It's our belief that God is dynamic and is always in communion with the created order. God through constant engagement with and through the created order is always engaged in the process of reviving, rectifying and restructuring God's image and likeness in the human order. This constant communion with and through God is what young people could be oriented to and grow into.

## Re- Building Scripture Concreteness Among Young People

> Our first task as youth ministers is to be with young people just as Jesus was with people. Our second task is to help youth develop the eyes, ears, and heart of Jesus for themselves. We're not only called to be witnesses among young people, we are also called, like Jesus, to be teachers. We're called to awaken youth to the presence of God in the world.[4]

Today one of the most used books in the world is the Bible, and one of the most misused books in the world is again the bible. Youth who consider Bible as literal revelation of God need to be empowered to understand it properly. It is the role of youth ministers to create space for learning, listening and dialogue with the scripture among young people so that they can find meaning and purpose for their lives. Bible has the potential to always read us, convict us, encourage us and prepare us for faithful action in this world. Unfortunately, there is little attempt to view biblical teachings in their entirety and understand the teachings as they were meant to be understood. Literal readings and superstitious beliefs about the Bible have taken deep roots in the minds of many young Christian believers. Space for careful study of the Bible with a proper understanding of the context and times during which the books of the Bible were written, as well as their relevance and applicablity in today's context should be dealt with carefully in the light of balancing biblical principles of justice and love.

## Reaffirming Jesus Christ as the Role Model

Jesus a young champion for the cause of justice and love stands as the epitome of Godself for all of us. His ever accepting and embracing nature, his compassionate kindness, love for the sick and vulnerable, his anger against forces of the empire which push people to margins are a source of inspiration specially to our young people. Jesus' invitation to the two disciples of John the Baptist to "come and see" is an invitation to experience God's hospitality, it's an invitation towards transparency, accountability and setting the house in order, it's an invite to come and witness what and who Jesus was… this confidence in Jesus ought to be the confidence of the church community in accepting the young and embracing them as they are. Just as the inhabitants of Nazareth were meeting the incarnated God on the streets, when working, having fun or with a glass of wine,[5] today the church needs to enable young people meet God in the form of Jesus Christ for inspiration and challenge not just within the four walls of the church but beyond them as well.

## Rethinking Ecclesia As the Context

Jesus in context is the church. Ecclesia or the church is the community of people who find meaning and add meaning to each other's existence. It is about "being" that church in the market place, in the streets and in the fringes of the society engaging with people in their struggles and in their insecurities, adding hope to their living, becoming vulnerable yet gathering strength in grace and humility. The church needs to prepare young people for this ecclesia called out to live faith in praxis. It is to recognize God's image and likeness in the created order and break the barriers of sacred and profane in faithful *diakonia* to which the church needs to lead the young people towards.

Understanding God's justice as the preferential option with the suffering masses and emulating Jesus who is the embodiment of truth are the starting points in our journey of rethinking ecclesia as young people. In this journey the church and the young people need to become vulnerable and engage in the praxis of diakonia not minding to dirty the white linen robes in witness and service.

Rethinking Ecclesia should recognize and nurture that freedom of thought and critical thinking among the young people. It is about giving them the choice to experience truth and justice in our own witness and service… inviting them to "come and see" for themselves… inviting us (as ecclesia) to set our lives and house in order. Seeking truth and practicing justice is not an end in itself but only a means towards reaching, recognizing and realizing that end in God's Kindom. It also entails asking the right questions and altering lifestyles with hope

Today for the sake of the gospel, we need to be the ecclesia which affirms the voice of constructive criticism and enables young people to engage in this progressive movement of faith journey so that they love the church and belong to the church as they re-envision a new and a better church for today and tomorrow.

## Endnotes

[1] Frantisek Stech, "Who are Youth in Theological Perspective," *Journal of Youth and Theology* Vol.15, 30 Sep 2016: 124-145. <file:///C:/Users/Admin/Downloads/Who_are_Youth_in_Theological_Perspective%20(1).pdf> (21 Dec 2019)

[2] Wesley W. Ellis, "Human Beings and Human Becomings: Departing from the Developmental Model of Youth Ministry," *Journal of Youth and Theology,* Vol. 14, No. 2 (2015): 119–137.

[3] Friedrich Schweitzer, "Adolescents as Theologians: a New Approach in Christian education and Youth ministry," Religious Education Vol. 109, No. 2 (2014): 185.

[4] Quote by Mark Yaconelli, Co-founder of Youth ministries and spirituality at San francisco theological seminary.

[5] Vladmir Boublik, *Meeting with Jesus* (Svitavy: Trinitas,2002), 127.

## Bibliography

Ellis, Wesley W. "Human Beings and Human Becomings: Departing from the Developmental Model of Youth

Ministry," *Journal of Youth and Theology,* Vol. 14, No. 2 (2015): 119–137.

Schweitzer, Friedrich. "Adolescents as Theologians: a New Approach in Christian education and Youth ministry." Page 185 in *Religious Education* Vol. 109, No. 2 (2014): 185

Stech, Frantisek. "Who are Youth in Theological Perspective," *Journal of Youth and Theology* Vol.15, 30 Sep 2016: 124-145.

<file:///C:/Users/Admin/Downloads/Who_are_Youth_in_Theological_Perspective%20(1).pdf> (21 Dec 2019)

Vladmir Boublik, *Meeting with Jesus.* Svitavy: Trinitas, 2002.

# Contributors

1. Rev. Dr. Vincent Vinod Kumar, Presbyter, CSI Karnataka Central Diocese, Bangalore
2. Mrs. Rebecca Azariah, Faculty, Gurukul Lutheran Theological College, Chennai
3. Rev. Dr. Praveen P.S. Perumalla, Auxiliary Secretary, Telengana Division, Bible Society of India
4. Rev. S Soban Kumar Daniel, Presbyter, CSI South Kerala Diocese
5. Rev. David Joseph Raj, Presbyter, CSI Kanyakumari Diocese
6. Rev. D. Isaac Devadoss, Associate Professor, Department of History of Christianity, Bishop's College, Kolkata.
7. Rev. Dr. V.J. John, Diocese of Kolkata, CNI, Professor of New Testament, Bishop's College, Kolkata, Dean of Doctoral Studies, North India Institute of Post-Graduate Theological Studies (NIIPGTS), President of the Society for Biblical Studies in India (SBSI).
8. Prof.Dr.Mathew Koshy Punnackad, (Rtd. Principal, Bishop Moore College, Mavelikara), Hon. Director, Department of Ecological Concerns, CSI Synod, Editor and Publisher of New Vision magazine

9. Revd Viji Varghese Eapen, Presbyter, CSI Madhya Kerala Diocese Research Student (PhD - Theology), School of Theology, Philosophy, and Music, Dublin City University, Dublin 9, Ireland
10. Rev. Jyothi Issac, Presbyter, CSI South Kerala Diocese
11. Rev. Dr. S. Samuel Rajadurai, Presbyter, CSI Trichy Tanjore Diocese
12. Rev. P. Ravi, Presbyter, CSI Thoothukudi-Nazareth Diocese
13. Rev. Christopher Rajkumar, Executive Secretary, NCCI - Unity and Mission, National Council of Churches in India,
14. Rev. K. S. Shaiju Kumar, Presbyter, CSI South Kerala Diocese
15. Rev. Vinod Allen, Presbyter, CSI Malabar Diocese, Faculty, KUTS
16. Rev. Solomon Paul. J, Director, Youth Department, CSI Synod

www.ingramcontent.com/pod-product-compliance
Ingram Content Group UK Ltd.
Pitfield, Milton Keynes, MK11 3LW, UK
UKHW041827200726
13854UKWH00002BA/613